Irish in Michigan

DISCOVERING THE PEOPLES OF MICHIGAN
Arthur W. Helweg, Russell M. Magnaghi, and Linwood H. Cousins, Series Editors

Ethnicity in Michigan: Issues and People
Jack Glazier and Arthur W. Helweg

Discovering the Peoples of Michigan is a series of publications examining the state's rich multicultural heritage. The series makes available an interesting, affordable, and varied collection of books that enables students and lay readers to explore Michigan's ethnic dynamics. A knowledge of the state's rapidly changing multicultural history has far-reaching implications for human relations, education, public policy, and planning. We believe that Discovering the Peoples of Michigan will enhance understanding of the unique contributions that diverse and often unrecognized communities have made to Michigan's history and culture.

Irish in Michigan

Seamus P. Metress and Eileen K. Metress

Michigan State University Press

East Lansing

♾ The paper used in this publication meets the minimum requirements
of ANSI/NISO Z39.48-1992 (R 1997) (Permanence of Paper).

Michigan State University Press
East Lansing, Michigan 48823-5245

Printed and bound in the United States of America.
12 11 10 09 08 07 06   1 2 3 4 5 6 7 8 9 10

LIBRARY OF CONGRESS CATALOGING-IN-PUBLICATION DATA
Metress, Seamus P.
Irish in Michigan / Seamus P. Metress and Eileen K. Metress.
p. cm.—(Discovering the peoples of Michigan)
Includes bibliographical references and index.
ISBN 0-87013-764-6 (pbk. : alk. paper) 1. Irish Americans—Michigan—History. 2. Irish
Americans—Michigan—Social conditions. 3. Immigrants—Michigan—History. 4.
Michigan—Ethnic relations. 5. Michigan—Social conditions. I. Metress, Eileen K. II. Title.
III. Series.
F575.I6M47 2006
977.400491'62—dc22
2006005186
Discovering the Peoples of Michigan. The editors wish to thank
the Kellogg Foundation for their generous support.

Cover design by Ariana Grabec-Dingman
Book design by Sharp Des!gns, Lansing, Michigan
Cover photo: Members of the Roddy, McCauley, and Gallagher families on Beaver Island
circa 1916. Courtesy of Beaver Island Historical Society.

Michigan State University Press is a member of the Green Press Initiative and is
committed to developing and encouraging ecologically responsible publishing
practices. For more information about the Green Press Initiative and the use of
recycled paper in book publishing, please visit *www.greenpressinitiative.org*.

Visit Michigan State University Press on the World Wide Web at *www.msupress.msu.edu*

We dedicate this work to the memory of Alec Marron, Dan O'Kennedy, Gerry Collins, Mike Melody, and Joe Myles, truer sons of Erin you'll not find. They dedicated their lives to the promotion of Irish culture and the freedom and unity of their ancestral home. We'll never see the likes of them again.

ACKNOWLEDGMENTS

The authors would like to thank Adela Rios for her patience and attention to detail in typing and proof-reading the manuscript. Her assistance was invaluable.

We would also like to thank the many friends and acquaintances of Irish ancestry in Michigan who have shared their stories and knowledge over the years.

SERIES ACKNOWLEDGMENTS

Discovering the Peoples of Michigan is a series of publications that resulted from the cooperation and effort of many individuals. The people recognized here are not a complete representation, for the list of contributors is too numerous to mention. However, credit must be given to Jeffrey Bonevich, who worked tirelessly with me on contacting people as well as researching and organizing material.

The initial idea for this project came from Mary Erwin, but I must thank Fred Bohm, director of the Michigan State University Press, for seeing the need for this project, for giving it his strong support, and for making publication possible. Also, the tireless efforts of Keith Widder and Elizabeth Demers, senior editors at Michigan State University Press, were vital in bringing DPOM to fruition.

Otto Feinstein and Germaine Strobel of the Michigan Ethnic Heritage Studies Center patiently and willingly provided names for contributors and constantly gave this project their tireless support. Yvonne Lockwood of the Michigan State University Museum has also suggested and advised contributors.

Many of the maps in the series were prepared by Gregory Anderson at the Geographical Information Center (GIS) at Western Michigan University under the directorship of David Dickason. Additional maps have been contributed by Ellen White.

Other authors and organizations provided comments on other aspects of the work. There are many people that were interviewed by the various authors who will remain anonymous. However, they have enabled the story of their group to be told. Unfortunately, their names are not available, but we are grateful for their cooperation.

Most of all, this work is a tribute to the writers who patiently gave their time to write and share their research findings. Their contributions are noted and appreciated. To them goes most of the gratitude.

ARTHUR W. HELWEG, *Series Co-editor*

Contents

Irish Emigration to America

Irish immigration to the United States can be divided into five general periods extending from 1640 to the present. They are the colonial, pre-starvation, great starvation, post-starvation, and post-independence periods. Immigration to the Great Lakes region and, more specifically, Michigan was differentially influenced during each of these times.

Colonial Period 1640–1815

During the colonial period, Irish emigration was dominated by artisans, shopkeepers, and small farmers from an Ulster Protestant background. Contrary to popular belief, the number of Catholics who left Ireland was also significant consisting of possibly 40 percent of the total Irish migration. About a half million Irish came during this period including a significant number of indentured workers who could be tortured, mutilated, and killed with no consequences for the perpetrators. Some Irish were taken as slaves to the West Indies after the Cromwellian Wars in the middle of the seventeenth century. As late as 1714, one can find Irish and African slaves offered for sale together. Transportation of prisoners to America for penal servitude was also common at this time. Many of the transportees were Irish and were taken to Georgia, which was founded as a prison colony.

The primary causes of voluntary immigration at this time were commercial restrictions on Irish economic development and religious discrimination against both Catholics and dissenters, such as Quakers and Presbyterians. For example, both Catholics and dissenters had to pay tithes to support the Anglican Church and were subject to penal laws limiting their religious and political rights. During the political agitation associated with the United Irish movement of the 1790s, over 60,000 Irish came to America possibly 20 percent of whom were Catholic.

At this time renting practices became more exploitative. Between 1740 and 1840 while the Irish population tripled, rents continued to rise. In order to pay the "rack" rents the best land was devoted to cash crops, which went to the landlord or his agent. During this period, families began to divide their tenant holdings into smaller and smaller parcels. So, many began to choose emigration to America over chronic poverty at home especially after America freed itself of British rule.

This wave of immigrants settled mainly in the Middle Atlantic States of Pennsylvania, Maryland, and Virginia, and the southeastern states of Georgia, North Carolina, and South Carolina. Ulster Irish Protestants primarily settled in Western Pennsylvania, Georgia, and South Carolina while the Catholic Irish settled in Maryland, North Carolina, and Virginia, as well as in Maine. These early Irish opened, explored, and settled the first America frontier. They worked as boatmen, traders, Indian fighters, farmers, explorers, and even lawyers.

Irish indentures often ran away to the mountains, changed their names and identities, and became especially suspicious of the government and strangers in general. It is estimated that in Philadelphia as many as 10 percent of them ran away. Today in the Appalachians, substantial numbers of mountain folk can trace their origins to those Irish who fled servitude.

It was during this period that the Irish first entered the Great Lakes by way of the Ohio River and Appalachian passes spreading north along the expanding frontier. After the War of 1812, the Irish were heavily represented in frontier military garrisons. In Michigan, John McNamara led the Fort Mackinac militia, which had been established by Indian traders in northwest Michigan.

The bulk of Ireland's earliest immigrants are often called Scotch-Irish by both scholars and the public. However, the term requires some explanation since it was not in common use until the 1850s long after the colonial period had ended. The term actually was coined by some Ulster Irish and their Anglo-American allies to differentiate themselves from the largely Catholic Irish masses who poured into America fleeing starvation. The latter were poor and mostly unskilled and viewed as belligerent and culturally deprived. The term Scotch-Irish reflected a bio-political construct that saw them as undesirable and unwelcome. It even perpetuated the notion that the Irish and Scotch-Irish were two separate "races."

The early Ulster Protestant settlers had called themselves Irish and were referred to as such by the Anglo-American establishment. These early settlers had joined Irish organizations such as the Friendly Sons of St. Patrick and the Hibernian Society, not Scottish ones. The parents of Andrew Jackson, our first Irish president, were Ulster protestants who emigrated from County Antrim. Jackson, born in 1767 in the midst of the colonial period, identified himself as Irish, was a member of the Hibernian society, and even professed an abiding hatred of the English establishment.

Complicating and further corrupting Irish identity is the fact that many former Catholic Irish and their descendents have been subsumed under the moniker Scotch-Irish. The latter designation is reserved for those who were Irish and Protestant or, at the least, non-Catholic. Many early Catholic Irish gave up their religion for various reasons. In many states, practicing Catholicism was dangerous or economically disadvantageous. Many southern states legislated that children be baptized Protestant and banned the existence of Catholic churches. Thus, many southern Catholics became Baptists.

Conversion was common due to repression and convenience. In Pennsylvania, Irish Catholics became Quakers in order to secure civil rights, while on the frontier where few Catholic churches existed they became Baptists and Methodists. In the early years especially on the frontier, intermarriage with Irish Protestants was not uncommon often resulting in the conversion of the Catholic.

The above examples help to explain why so many "Scotch-Irish," nay Irish American Protestants, bear traditionally Catholic surnames such as Kelly, McDonagh, Ryan, and Sullivan. Confusion is further perpetuated when some scholars identify persons with such names as Scotch-Irish. Many who write in this area appear not to have a solid conception of what constitutes an Irish name or the variety of ways that such names were Anglicized both in Ireland and America.

The earliest Irish immigrants so often labeled as Scotch-Irish had a great impact on America. Their members opened the great frontier, founded American Presbyterianism, excelled in the field of education, and achieved much political success. Their numbers included Francis Mckemie, the founder of the American Presbyterian church, as well as Presidents Jackson, Buchanan, Arthur, Polk, McKinley, and Wilson. They Americanized readily and in most areas rapidly became socioculturally indistinguishable from the mainstream, thus losing their identity. However, in some areas such as the isolated parts of Appalachia they survive culturally. There the people, the surnames, the musical instruments, the songs, the airs, and the dances bespeak an Irish or Celtic origin. Interestingly, in the 1990 census, hundreds of thousands of descendants of Ulster Protestants who settled in the South chose the category Irish not Scotch-Irish to indicate their ethnicity.

Pre-Starvation Period 1815–1845

The pre-starvation period began in the wake of a world wide economic depression following the Napoleonic Wars in 1815. Between 1815 and 1845 it is estimated that 1,000,000 Irish immigrants settled in eastern cities like New York, Philadelphia, and Boston, as well as inland along the canal routes. Although most became urban pioneers, others settled down as farmers or in small towns along the canal routes. Initially, the majority were Ulster Protestants, but later massive numbers of Catholics came from all over Ireland. It was during this period that the canal system provided speedier routes through the Great Lakes region. The Irish who built most of the canals had dug almost 4,000 miles in

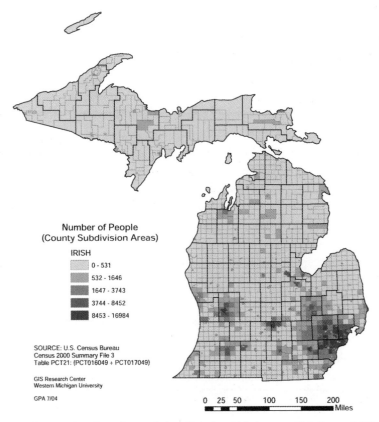

Number of People
(County Subdivision Areas)

IRISH

0 - 531
532 - 1646
1647 - 3743
3744 - 8452
8453 - 16984

SOURCE: U.S. Census Bureau
Census 2000 Summary File 3
Table PCT21: (PCT016049 + PCT017049)

GIS Research Center
Western Michigan University

GPA 7/04

0   25   50   100   150   200
                                    Miles

Distribution of Michigan's Population Claiming Irish Ancestry, U.S. Census 2000.

the Eastern United States by 1850. Many of them perished but many more settled in communities along the way. Michigan was opened at this time to a slow but constant stream of immigrants from Ireland.

Charles O'Malley from County Mayo migrated to Michigan in 1836. He helped to establish an Irish settlement on Mackinac Island. By 1840 he owned a successful general store. In 1846 he was elected as a Mackinac County representative to the Michigan legislature. He was responsible for the Irish names given to the northern Michigan counties of Roscommon, Wexford, Clare, Emmet, and Antrim.[1]

At this time in Ireland the end of the Napoleonic Wars resulted in the partial loss of English markets for Irish agricultural products, as well as further restrictions by the crown on Irish industrialization. At the same time, a shift from tillage to grazing encouraged estate clearance by eviction of small farmers and peasants. Furthermore, agrarian secret societies, such as the Whiteboys, were beginning to use violence and intimidation to deal with oppressive landlords and their agents, as well as resisting the tithes payable to the Anglican Church. Fear of becoming caught up in such violence concerned many people.

These many factors led to a great exodus to America for those in search of a safer, more secure, and democratic way of life. At this time, more and more American ships were carrying raw materials to England and on their return voyages offered cheap passage to America. The immigrants served as paying ballast and could rearrange themselves on demand to keep the ship upright as conditions at sea changed.

The Great Starvation 1845–1855

Irish immigration to America was already well underway before the start of the Great Starvation, which initiated a period of emigration that turned loose possibly 1 to 1½ million emigrants largely from the west and southwest of Ireland. These individuals were the most destitute and possibly the most illiterate of all Irish immigrants.

They left hurriedly by any means available including overcrowded, unseaworthy "coffin" ships. These ships were characterized by a death rate similar to that of slave ships out of Africa. The people who came at this time had awesome memories of suffering, death, and racist oppression at the hands of England.

Many had no choice but to leave due to evictions and the possibility of death by starvation or related diseases. The failure of the potato crop left the Irish peasants in many areas of the country without food, since the cash crops they had raised belonged to the landlord or his agent. The social structure of rural Ireland collapsed as families died or were broken up. The British response based on faulty economic theory and violent anti-Irish racism was for the most part one of inaction. Government relief operations when they existed were minimal, too late, and vindictive. Many lost everything and watched death all around them. It is estimated that over 1½ to 2 million died.

Beaver Island Fishermen prior to 1916. Courtesy of Beaver Island Historical Society.

Throughout the years of starvation, Irish food was exported to England. In the early years there was enough food to feed all of Ireland but the cash crops belonging to the landlords were not made available to the Irish people who labored to raise them. In fact, a strong case can be made for opportunistic genocide against the Irish people by the actions and inactions of their English overlords.

The immigrants of this era settled heavily in the cities of the eastern seaboard but great numbers spread first along canal and later along railroad routes. The Irish settled in cities like Akron, Buffalo, Chicago, Cleveland, St. Louis, St. Paul, San Francisco, Toledo, Memphis, and Butte. In fact, Butte, Montana, became the most Irish city in America in the late nineteenth century.

A significant number of Irish settlers eventually spread out into farming and mining communities throughout the rural west and Midwest. At this time, many moved into the Detroit metropolitan area, as well as into farming areas throughout Michigan. In the 1840s, a number of Irish took up fishing in places like Beaver Island, Mackinac Island, Bay City, Saginaw, and Alpena. From 1853 to 1854, Irish

Celtic Cross at the entry of St. Patrick's Cemetery, Parnell, erected in memory of Father E.J. "James Byrne," a former pastor. Courtesy of Pat Nugent, St. Patrick's Parish historian.

emigrants from the Great Starvation dug the Sault Ste. Marie Canal while others dug canals in Grand Rapids and Saginaw. From the Copper country of the north to Beaver Island, Irishtown in Gratiot County, Parnell in Kent County, Lenawee County, southeast Allegan County, and Niles in the south, Irish people established themselves in rural areas.

Post-Starvation Period 1855–1920s

Emigration continued after the Great Starvation. Between 1855 and the 1920s, another 2,500,000 came to the United States again largely from the west and southwest of Ireland. This group was the most educated due to the development of the National school system. As a group, they sent massive amounts of money home to improve the conditions of those left behind or to pay for further emigration. They came to previously settled areas with established Irish communities. However, this was the great period of railroad building, mining, and homesteading. Thus, many followed or worked railroad lines into the interior of the United States. The Great Starvation institutionalized emigration as a way of life for the Irish. The young grew up knowing that they would emigrate. There was little or no prospect for work and land was no longer being divided among families. There was little left to divide. Prospects for inheriting land were now limited and resulted in less frequent and later marriages. When the former did occur, there were few prospective mates in one's own age range. Women had fewer prospects for jobs or marriage in Ireland. Hence, single female emigration was heavy.

At this time, economic conditions were again deteriorating with an increase in evictions and a threat of famine or at least significant food shortages. Political repression by England was increasing especially after the Fenian uprising and the Land War that followed. Agrarian violence and civil disobedience were growing during the Land War against landlordism. The build up toward a crisis over home rule and the eventual war of liberation between 1918 and 1921 led to further repression. Some wished to escape the violence and repression that often accompanied it—an unfree Ireland was once again in trouble.

The Irish coming to Michigan during this period worked building railroads.[2] The jobs were dirty and dangerous and the employers were exploitative, but the Irish flocked to the opportunities for work. After building the railroad, the Irish began to run it. Railroad workers were tough and quite ready to fight for their rights. The Irish rank and file became committed to labor unions and developed a core of radical militants. The railroads, like canals, gave the Irish mobility both geographically and economically. The work also gave them a sense of self worth as they contributed to the development of their new country.

During the Civil War, the Fifteenth Michigan Infantry was known as the "Irish" Regiment. They distinguished themselves in the Mississippi Valley campaign of 1862–63 and the Battles of Pittsburg Landing, Shiloh, Corinth, and Vicksburg. They also participated in Sherman's March to the Sea.[3] Bridget Divers who accompanied her husband to war rallied the first Michigan Cavalry at the Battle of Fair Oaks after her husband was wounded.[4] It is estimated that 4,000 Irish-born and many more American Irish Michiganders served in the Union Army. Further, Fr. William Corby gained great fame and respect as chaplain for the fabled Irish Brigade. Corby later became the president of the University of Notre Dame.

The Irish participated in the Great Lakes lumber industry between 1870 and 1920. Many of them took up employment in the woods and hills of Michigan, Wisconsin, and Minnesota. The sawmill towns they often created disappeared after World War I, which led many of them into manufacturing or onto the docks and ships of the lakes.

In 1889, 112,000 men worked the woods at 20–30 dollars a week in the Great Lakes.[5] Lumberjacks were tough, hard working men who lived and worked under horrendous conditions in the northwoods. Among these men were legendary Irish lumberjacks like "Silver Jack" John Driscoll and Jack McGovern who worked the Michigan woods from Saginaw Bay to Muskegon. These two were tough fighting men employed by the lumber companies to get their logs down the river past rivals.[6]

Some Irish in the north of Michigan practiced dairy and potato farming, while dependent on work in the woods or sawmills. When the woods shut down, farms were lost and settlers left. In southern Michigan, the Irish dug drainage ditches, tiled farm fields, and built railroads and roads, while substantial numbers took up farming. Many of their descendents remain on the land today.

Post-Independence Period 1920s–Present

Since the conclusion of the Anglo Irish War in 1921 and the partition of Ireland into two parts, the emigration pattern has been one of spurts and lulls. Shortly after the founding of the Irish Free State, emigration slowed dramatically. The Irish Civil War, which was fought over partition, led to some emigration of dissidents from the anti-treaty Irish Republican Army (IRA). However, emigration from the six northeastern counties still under British occupation continued for the nationalist community. The discriminatory nature of the partitioned statelet with respect to employment, housing, and civil rights encouraged greater emigration from the northeast. Detroit was especially affected by such migration. It was many of these emigrants who became heavily involved in the revival of Irish Nationalist political activity in Michigan after the fall of the Civil Rights Movement in northeast Ireland.

It was during this period that future labor leaders who were members of the anti-treaty IRA, like Mike Quill in New York and Pat Quinn and Pat Rice in Detroit, emigrated to America. Quill founded the Transport Workers Union (TWU) in New York while Quinn along with Pat Rice was important in the development of the United Auto Workers (UAW) as one of America's most powerful unions.

Harlan Hatcher, of the University of Michigan, once said that the Irish were the "bone and sinew of the lake states."[7] They deepened and smoothed harbors. They also worked on the docks and the boats on the lakes. They drained the swamps, tiled the fields, and cleared the land. They excavated and built the early canals and roads with sheer muscle power and later constructed the railroad grades and tracks in the same manner. Later they became key operatives in the growing manufacturing sector where they were involved in union organization as well as local community development.

In the 1980s legal and illegal emigration, especially among the young, again increased from the Republic of Ireland due to severe economic problems at home. It is estimated that there could have been as many as 300,000 to 500,000 illegal Irish in the United States working in an "off the books" economy in bars, domestic work, and construction. Michigan became a home for a number of these illegal refugees from economic hard times. Most recently the 26-county state of Ireland has experienced an economic boom referred to as "The Celtic Tiger." This has led to a slowing of emigration and the return of many Irish exiles to seek employment at home. How long this situation will continue in a fluctuating world economy remains to be seen.

The Urban Irish in Detroit

The summer of 2001 marked the 300th birthday of the city of Detroit. Edsel Ford, great-grandson of Henry Ford and Chairman of Detroit's anniversary commemoration, credited the city's strength to its ethnic diversity. Underscoring his own Irish-American heritage he noted that "The Irish have been, and continue to be, significant contributors to the vitality of Detroit."[8] In further celebration of Detroit's birthday and in remembrance of the many Irish who left home to eventually find refuge within its confines, the United Irish Societies prepared the following Irish Heritage Statement:

> Irish immigrants came to Detroit—some, reluctant exiles fleeing famine and oppression; others, in search of freedom and opportunity—all armed with an enduring faith in God, a keen Irish wit, and a restless spirit that left them yearning for their beloved Emerald Isle.[9]

Their trip to Detroit from Ireland was a long, often arduous one, frequently involving one or more stops along the way. They trickled in at first to the frontier that was Detroit. Some came from Canada, others from places, like New York and Boston, along America's eastern seaboard. The number of Irish who came to Detroit significantly grew throughout the early 1800s. By 1850, they represented the city's largest immigrant group. They came in search of jobs and higher wages and to flee the prejudice encountered elsewhere.

The Early Years

The Catholic religion, which identified the vast majority of Irish immigrants, did not elicit scorn on the streets of early Detroit. Detroit began as a Catholic town, a settlement of the old French Empire, a sequel to a fortified outpost of French Canada founded in the summer of 1701. The British captured it in 1760 during the French and Indian War. They held it until it became part of the United States in 1796. Yet, the French influence remained. When the Irish began to arrive they found an established parish where they could attend mass. For a time, the French church Ste. Anne's would be their church too. Detroit was a place to which both Catholics and Protestants could come without the expectation of religious hostilities endemic to so many locales in the early years of the United States and Canada.

Detroit's growth was tied to its geography. It was remote, located west of North America's early settlements. It also was tucked north on the edge of a peninsula within the configuration of the Great Lakes. The voyageurs had called the 29-mile stretch of water on which the city now sits "le détroit"—the strait. That strait, the Detroit River, flowing south connects Lake St. Claire with Lake Erie and along with the St. Claire River to the north links the Upper with the Lower Great Lakes. Detroit's location on its banks would make it a nineteenth-century transportation hub, a center for trade, and the nation's doorway to the Upper Lakes and their resources.

Before its promise could be achieved, the area needed to be accessible and to attract more people. Developments in the early 1800s would help to achieve both. In 1818, the steamboat Walk-in-the-Water sailed into Detroit from Buffalo taking only a few days. Its arrival marked a significant date in the peopling of Michigan and began a new period of rapid travel west. Never before had Michigan been so close to the eastern states.[10]

The year of the ship's maiden voyage coincided with the opening of the area's first land office. Cheap land would draw people west. By 1822, 20,000 acres had been sold.[11] One such buyer was Daniel Corby, who bought land and built a home. He was like of many of the Irish who came to North America in the early 1800s. Coming mostly from Ireland's eastern counties, the emigrants tended to be more prosperous arriving with skills and education. Corby, for example, had left his native county Offaly as a young man and sailed to Quebec. There he met his wife. Within a few years, in 1826, they moved to Detroit where he worked in real estate and civil engineering. His family name was to become a part of American history. One of his sons, Fr. William Corby, would be immortalized as the priest who administered absolution to the troops at the Battle of Gettysburg in 1863.

The importance of the Great Lakes and Detroit to the country's interior development was marked by the completion of the Erie Canal in 1825. It is heralded as one of the most significant factors in Michigan's development. Waterfalls and rapids east of Lake Erie were obstacles to a continuous water route east. Now, a canal stretching over 360 miles across New York state from Buffalo to the Hudson River provided that connection. The canal, which took ten years to complete, was dug largely by Irish immigrant laborers. It opened the way for the exploitation of resources in the hinterlands, commercial transport from throughout the Great Lakes, and the establishment of a population base. People were needed to process, manufacture, and distribute raw materials, finished goods, and agricultural products. And the Irish emigrants needed work.

With the canal's completion, immigrants began to stream into the area. Detroit was growing and the infrastructure needed to support it would too. Many of the Irish who had worked on the canal found Detroit a hospitable place in which to take up residence. Likewise, for those who wished to flee the anti-Irish biases of America's east coast, the social climate of Detroit with its promise of jobs attracted them like a magnet. Throughout the 1820s and 1830s they began to move west, many in response to newspaper ads and posters announcing a wide range of employment opportunities. Recruits were needed to build docks and warehouses, railways and terminals, roads, and more.

Robert Elliott arrived in 1834. Born in County Tipperary, he was an architect-builder who had met employment discrimination in his native Ireland. Knowing that his Catholicism would remain a life-long obstacle in spite of his education and training, he left for Quebec in 1819. There he encountered the same religious bigotry from powerful Anglicans. He relocated to upstate New York where he worked until that area's economic hard times brought him and his family to Detroit.

In six years, Elliott would die in an accident at a construction site.[12] In those few short years before that tragic event, he made a powerful name for himself. Elliott's broad-based popularity was underscored when not long before his death he was elected associate judge for Wayne County. He left a lasting mark with one of his final acts—the establishment of the Elliott Emigration Office. As a business that would eventually arrange passage for thousands of European immigrants to Detroit, it continued and flourished after Elliott's death under the able direction of his son Richard.

When the senior Elliott arrived, Detroit was still a rather primitive outpost of nineteenth-century America. Change, however, was on the horizon. In the 1840s, significant deposits of iron ore were discovered in Michigan's upper peninsula. Likewise, the commercial extraction and refinement of copper ore, long known to be there, began. Detroit would benefit. The city was situated on a water route in direct line to receive these raw materials and it had a population base to accommodate their transformation into products and profits. By the mid-1840s, iron furnaces, smelters, foundries, factories, and sawmills were putting more Detroiters to work, Irishmen included. Detroit was becoming a center of heavy industry.

Toward the decade's end, Detroit absorbed another cohort of Irish immigrants hoping to make a better future within its boundaries, those who had fled Erin in the midst of famine. Ireland's Great Starvation sent millions to their graves and hordes of its surviving peasants to North America. Unless they knew someone who sponsored their journey inland, the starving Irish who came to Detroit did so in a series of haphazard stops along the way. Arriving inexperienced and without resources, the vast majority found work as laborers. However, the hardest, lowest paying, and often most dangerous work was never reserved for the Irish as was the case on the east coast. In Detroit, people from various ethnic groups labored side by side. Work was available commensurate with one's ability not one's ethnicity.

Thus, by the mid-nineteenth century, the city's largest immigrant group was represented in various occupations. Some were laborers. Others owned businesses, such as small shops, groceries, and bars. Some worked as dray men hauling coal, wood, and freight to and from the docks and rail yards with their own wagons and horses. Others were painters, plasterers and carpenters. Some were professionals—judges, doctors, and architects.[13]

Sometimes women and children worked too usually in jobs that promised to be more steadily available than those of many Irish laboring men.[14] They worked in the clothing industry turning out the rugged boots and garments worn by those who toiled in Michigan's hinterlands. Some were clerks or domestics. Daughters might have worked in private homes as hired girls. Together with children, women worked in tobacco factories usually making cigars.[15] In most cases, neither married Irish women nor their children worked full-time. Their earnings added to the family income when times were most difficult. Some women did run boarding houses providing rooms and meals and a sense of home and family for those who lived under their roofs.[16]

Early Corktown and Holy Trinity Church

Detroit's most concentrated area of Irish settlement in the mid-nineteenth century was the Eighth Ward's "Corktown." Subdivided in 1835, its houses sat on what was once French farmland that ran north of the Detroit River "as far north as a horse could plow in one day."[17] Third and Eighth Streets marked Corktown's eastern and western boundaries, the river and what is now the Vernor Highway its southern and northern edges.

During the 1820s and 1830s when the Irish began arriving in Detroit in significant numbers, most of them rented in what is now downtown Detroit. Unlike in the eastern cities where space was severely limited, people did not congregate in high rises. Here there was room for expansion out of the congestion and movement west to the city's Eighth Ward soon began.

The 1850s saw a substantial increase in Detroit's Irish population, the Eighth Ward disproportionately so. For those Irish who lived in the Ward of their greatest assemblage, there was much to remind them of Ireland. Accents, old ways, and stories of home were never farther than next door! But indeed, within the Ward's boundaries, the Irish tended to live in enclaves according to their counties of origin—Cork, Kerry, Limerick, and Tipperary.[18]

Corktown was chiefly a residential neighborhood close to industry, businesses, and jobs along the river. Life there was much the same for its residents regardless of their ethnicity for not everyone who lived there was Irish. Indeed, at this time, half of them were not Irish. Extended families, boarders, and sometimes multiple families lived under one roof. Likewise, according to major social indicators, the Ward's Irish residents were not unlike their compatriots who lived elsewhere in mixed ethnic neighborhoods scattered throughout the city.

However, at mid-century, Corktown came to house what was and would continue to be the essence of Irish Catholicism in Detroit—Most Holy Trinity Church. Holy Trinity literally came to rest there after being placed on logs and rolled fifteen blocks from Bates and Cadillac Square in the town's center to the corner of Sixth and Porter Streets in Corktown. With its move in 1849, the church had followed many of the Irish to the Eighth Ward. The significance of that move is tied to Holy Trinity's history as the Irish church and the first English-speaking urban Catholic church in the "western states." If its history at that time was not long, it was elaborate.

Like other early Catholic immigrants to Detroit, the Irish had continued to worship at Ste. Anne's whose capacity to accommodate them was now taxed. The Irish needed a church of their own where they could all fit, where they were not relegated to special masses, and where the sermons were delivered in English. The Irish Catholics of Detroit would have their own church in 1834 due to the efforts of Alpheus White. Before coming to Detroit, White had fought in the Battle of New Orleans serving as first lieutenant in the exclusively Irish Fifth Company under the command of his brother. An architect, White left Louisiana and moved to Cincinnati before moving on to Detroit. Shortly after his arrival, he purchased an old frame church from the First Protestant

Society of Detroit and moved it to a lot he owned at Bates and Cadillac. There he remodeled it for the Irish Catholic community and dedicated the building as Holy Trinity Church.[19]

Before the renovation could be completed, a cholera epidemic struck the city. Fr. Martin Kundig, a Detroit priest at the time, played a leadership role in dealing with the situation. White turned the building over to him for use as a makeshift hospital, fashioning needed changes and neglecting his own business in the process. White assisted Fr. Kundig and parishioners in caring for the cholera victims.[20] Fr. Kundig was recognized for his heroic efforts in helping the sick and dying, spending much of his time transporting them from Detroit's streets to the church turned temporary hospital. When the epidemic subsided, the church was remodeled and dedicated on Trinity Sunday, 1835. Its first pastor was Fr. Bernard O'Cavanagh and its second was Fr. Kundig.

During that same year, White was appointed a Wayne County delegate to the convention, which framed Michigan's first constitution in its application for statehood. White convinced its members to grant voting rights to Michigan's foreign-born residents. The following year he was made artillery commander of Michigan troops in the Territorial militia's bloodless Toledo War. In 1838, White returned to Cincinnati. He died there presumably due to the effects of a rifle ball he had carried in his body since leaving Louisiana after the war.[21] Though his stay in Michigan was brief, he left a lasting impact not the least of which was the establishment of Holy Trinity church.

In 1844, the cornerstone was laid for Detroit's new cathedral Sts. Peter and Paul built at the direction of Bishop Peter Paul Lefevere. Consecrated in 1848, it unseated Ste. Anne's as the principal church of the diocese. The large, new building also absorbed the congregation of Holy Trinity whose numbers were outpacing the old church's size. Holy Trinity was closed and its records transferred to the new cathedral. However, as the mid-century influx of Irish immigrants added to Corktown's population, the inconvenience of travel to and from the cathedral was magnified. Thus, Holy Trinity parish was revived and the old structure moved to Corktown.[22] Sts. Peter and Paul continued to serve central Detroit and the east side. The old building, bought and transformed by Alpheus White and lovingly moved to Corktown, was soon torn down. Construction on a new building began in 1855. The Irish church was now firmly anchored in Detroit's Irish section.

St. Peter's Episcopal Church located at Trumball and Michigan served many of Corktown's Irish Protestants. William Maybury was one of them. Later in the century Maybury would become a leading political figure serving two terms in the U.S. Congress and as Mayor of Detroit. A statue of him now stands in Grand Circus Park. His father Thomas had emigrated from County Cork. The parents of Henry Ford, William (also a native of Cork) and Mary O'Hern Ford, were married at St. Peter's and held their wedding reception in Corktown at the home of Thomas Maybury. The Fords frequently traveled from their farm in Greenfield Township to visit friends in the Eighth Ward. Their son Henry lived for a time with his aunt who was a member of St. Peter's.[23]

Nativism: The School Dispute of 1853–55

Detroit was not a town fraught with political strife or internecine warfare. For the most part its varied groups got along. Throughout its history Detroit had economically incorporated the waves of Irish immigrants who had made their way there.

The Know-Nothing Movement and the conflict between immigrants and nativists endemic to so many other American cities did not seriously plague Detroit. In many other places violence reigned with shootings, rioting, and the burning of Catholic churches and other properties. Not so in Detroit. The resentment of immigrants, however, was not totally absent. A small faction within the Whig party watched and resented the immigrant presence and their Catholicism.

This tension materialized in Detroit's infamous school dispute of 1853–55. A number of proposals in Detroit promised to increase expenses for the Catholic Church. One such proposal was the issuance of a paving tax on all roadside properties including those of the previously exempt Church. Outraged, Bishop Lefevere led a campaign to obtain tax support for the Catholic schools.

Parochial schools were of tremendous importance to most of the immigrant and ethnic Irish. These schools were more than a vehicle for educating and reinforcing religious beliefs. They were emblematic of the freedom enjoyed in America. Here they had the right to educate their children and to openly practice their Catholicism both of which had been too often denied them in their own homeland under British rule. Their schools would be maintained whatever the cost. The previous decade had seen the establishment of government supported elementary education. In 1842, the state legislature had approved a property tax to fund the public schools. Fr. Kundig and Cornelius O'Flynn, city attorney for Detroit as well as a native of County Kerry and a resident of Corktown, were among those who worked tirelessly toward its passage. Dollars were not earmarked for Catholic schools. The intent of the effort, theirs included, was to improve the very bad state of public education in Detroit. To that end a meeting was convened and was chaired by Dr. Zina Pitcher and Fr. Kundig. Interestingly, that meeting was to be the springboard for the Detroit Board of Education, which was created in 1842.[24]

The mission to support public education was not without its detractors. Many had considered it far too expensive. Ten years later it remained a controversial matter. Now, the suggestion that Catholic schools be funded too made the issue even more controversial. Some Catholics had maintained all along that it was unfair that they paid for public schools through their taxes while also seeing to the financial support of the Church-run schools to which they sent their own children. They argued that their tax dollars should be allocated to their church-operated schools.

Nativists were not concerned with debating the fairness of that concept. They fanned the flames of suspicion regarding the very existence of such schools. Whereas to the Irish parochial schools represented the freedom of America, the Nativists cautioned that their purpose was to undermine that freedom. The state issue was centered in Detroit. Bishop Lefevere led the proponents with Wayne County state representative Jeremiah O'Callaghan attempting to push it through the legislature. Rev. George Duffield of Detroit's First Presbyterian Church led the opposition. In the end, the legislature's Education Committee denied the request to consider the allocation of state monies to Catholic schools. Lefevere continued the fight unsuccessfully by attempting to favorably influence Detroit's School Board. The plan was to support sympathetic candidates to the Board in the 1853 election who might then allocate the requested funds. That effort also failed.

The former stability of the city was shaken. Catholics feared the future of church supported education, while Protestants feared a "papish conspiracy." Much of the press coverage was vitriolic and contributed to sectarian polarization and fear. It was in this environment that the *Catholic Vindicator* was born. A weekly newspaper, it provided a voice for expression and a defense against the opposition. Businessman Richard Elliott was an important financial contributor to its publication.

In reality, not all Catholics, Irish Catholics included, had supported state dollars for parochial schools. Their reasons were varied. Some feared losing control of the schools to the state. For some, a negative vote was a way of registering their opposition to Lefevere, a figure some viewed as overbearing and manipulative. There was also fear of economic repercussions. Leaders, not the city's rank and file, had raised the inflammatory issue. Maybe Protestant employers thus agitated would hire and fire accordingly at their will.[25]

Though the controversy soon faded, subsequent battles over the schools would reemerge. In 1890, the Detroit Board of Education heard a motion that would require all of its teachers to hold a public school education. Thirty years later, Bishop Michael Gallagher would lead successful campaigns against Michigan constitutional amendments that sought to eliminate private schools. The first such campaign was proposed in 1920 by Nativists in Wayne County. The Bishop united Catholics, Dutch Reformed groups, Lutherans, and Seventh Day Adventists, all of whom had their own schools, in its defeat. The issue was again quelled in 1924 when it resurfaced at the instigation of the Ku Klux Klan (KKK).[26]

Railroad Cars and Stoves

As America became embroiled in the Civil War, many from Detroit's Irish community became soldiers fighting in various battles, including those at Manassas and Gettysburg.[27] The war also generated jobs and industrial expansion bringing more Irish to Detroit.

In the years to come, Detroit's financial gains in manufacturing and industry would oscillate. Its geographic location tucked between the lakes cut it off from the commercial east-west flow enjoyed by Cleveland and Chicago. At the time of the Civil War, Detroit seemed destined to be the nation's iron and steel producing center, but eventually that post would go to Pittsburgh with the area around Chicago also reaping benefits.

Detroit, however, would continue to profit from its links to mining and the production of associated goods. Iron and steel ran the city's economy. Its earliest heavy industry was the manufacture of railroad cars and wheels along with various pieces of equipment. Work generated by such industry dated back to the 1840s and the arrival of large numbers of Irish immigrants. For a time, the city was the main center for the production of the Pullman Sleeping Car.[28] By the 1880s Detroit was the largest overall manufacturer of railroad cars and wheels in the country.

Detroit also became known as the nation's stove capital. The Dwyer brothers were intimately involved with the city's designation as such. These sons of Irish immigrants came to be counted among Detroit's leading businessmen and industrialists. Along with his brother James, Jeremiah Dwyer opened the Detroit Stove Works. The business grew and became the Michigan Stove Company in 1871 with Jeremiah as one of its principle owners. James, on the other hand, became an owner of Peninsular Stove Company. For over half a century, stove making was Detroit's leading industry.[29]

By the 1880s, Detroit's Irish population had doubled from what it had been at mid-century. During the 1880s, it would double again. The Irish population of Corktown would swell to greater numbers and spill out making its borders less distinct. However, during the same time period, the Irish were replaced by the Germans as Detroit's largest immigrant group. The Germans later would be eclipsed by the Poles. The Irish were soon to become "old Detroit."[30]

The Cause of Labor

As the nineteenth century was winding down, the labor movement was growing across the nation just as it was in Detroit. And the Irish were very much a part of it. In Detroit they were among the leaders in the trade union movement and they headed Knights of Labor assemblies. Before becoming a Michigan Democratic state senator, Bernard O'Reilly, from County Westmeath, organized and headed the ship carpenter's assembly. Strikes occurred throughout the 1880s and into the 1890s in various industries.[31] Employer attempts to end union activity, however, were well underway. As the twentieth century began, Detroit was declared a non-union or open-shop town by its major employers. Thus, a job was not contingent upon union membership.

In the early decades of the twentieth century, Detroit underwent an industrial metamorphosis. One of its own, Irish-American Henry Ford, revolutionized the manufacture of automobiles by developing their assembly line mass production. He is also recognized for introducing into his plant the eight-hour shift and a wage that exceeded the standard for the time. The availability of automobiles was no longer limited to the rich and their manufacture would spawn jobs. Employment would spring not only from their assembly but from the many related industries tied to their manufacture and maintenance. Propelled by the automobile industry, iron and steel would make a comeback.

In the ensuing years, a succession of immigrant workers from the British Isles and Ireland began to arrive in the United States. Many came to Detroit. They came with a level of sophistication that had been spawned by the society they left. They were survivors of political and economic upheaval and, in Ireland, violent insurrection. Many were skilled workers with a background in trade unionism and a strong sense of class consciousness. They would be instrumental in the development of the United Auto Workers (UAW) and in leading Detroit's largest and most militant UAW locals. Many of the early labor combatants were English, Scottish, Welsh, and Irish.

Upon arrival, they found the open-shop environment loathsome to their sensibilities. Back home union membership was a requirement for securing a job. Organizing workers became a priority. Those in the skilled trades became the keystone not only of automobile production but of worker solidarity in general. Millwrights, lathe hands, toolmakers, and fitters possessed skills essential to automobile production and unlike those on the assembly line, they were not easily replaced. They made parts and built and maintained the devices necessary for assembly. In fraternity with line workers, they could drive or shut-down production. Their role was augmented after the mid-1920s when Ford introduced the Model A requiring that plants be completely retooled. In 1930, General Motors began making automobile models that changed each year necessitating annual retooling. Their bargaining leverage was not seriously threatened when machines were first introduced to replace some of them. They were still needed to manufacture and set up the devices. The retooling practice, however, did alter their roles, creating the fear of an uncertain future and making for an explosive workforce.[32]

The 1930s were turbulent times in labor history. Relations were not always as congenial as in the early days of that first Ford plant. In the sometimes bitter and often hard fought battles, workers from Detroit's Irish community were well represented. Among them was Cornelius Patrick Quinn. Born in County Donegal, Pat Quinn had joined the Irish Republican Army at age 17, raided police barracks during Ireland's Black and Tan wars, and had been imprisoned by the newly formed Irish government for opposing the partition of Ireland. Released after six months, he sailed for Montreal in 1924 and was boarding in Corktown two years later.

In 1937, Quinn was a leader of the sit-down strike at the Dodge Main Plant of the Chrysler Corporation on Detroit's east side. Varyingly referred to as General Quinn or the Chief of Police, he was called upon to establish discipline and security. Quinn's experience in Ireland was viewed as an asset in flushing out and dealing with traitors and in confronting the state. He went on to become the first president of the UAW's Dodge Local 3—the largest single plant UAW local in the country—and president of the Wayne County Congress of Industrial Organizations (CIO) Council.[33]

Michael Magee, Pat Rice, Jack Thompson, and Hugh Thompson are among other Irish-born figures who gained prominence in various aspects of Detroit's labor activities. Jack Thompson, a veteran of the Irish labor movement, moved to Ohio where he became involved in Toledo's famed 1934 Auto Lite strike.[34]

Playing a much noted but vastly different role in a labor dispute was Michigan Democratic governor Frank Murphy. Murphy had held and would hold many different offices including judge, mayor of Detroit, U.S. Governor of the Philippines, and U.S. Attorney General under President Franklin Roosevelt, who nominated him as a U.S. Supreme Court Justice. Throughout his long career, Murphy demonstrated himself to be a humanitarian and true friend of the common people. He had campaigned for governor in 1936 on a pro-labor ticket declaring that were he a wage earner he would be a union member. Coinciding with his inauguration was the auto industry's first major sit-down strike, which occurred in Flint where Chevrolet and Fisher Body employees held control of the factories from December 1936 until February 1937.

General Motors requested that Murphy mobilize the National Guard, which he did. However, it was not to break the strike but to maintain order. Thus, he was instrumental in the signing of the first labor contract between the newly formed UAW-CIO and a major automobile corporation. With the signed contract, General Motors had grudgingly agreed to recognize the union as sole bargaining agent. Other sit-downs followed, including the apex at the Dodge Main Plant. Some sit-downs were mere shows of solidarity. All, however, were disruptive and served to energize unorganized workers in various types of jobs, from auto worker to retail clerk. The courts eventually ruled the sit-down illegal but due to their influence, Detroit was no longer an open-shop town.[35]

Opponents branded Murphy's refusal to suppress Flint's strike as treasonable. The House Committee on Un-American Activities held hearings to investigate his actions. Witnesses claimed that he was backed by Soviet agents and that his reelection would be disastrous for Michigan. Red-baiting, however, had not convinced Detroit. In his next bid for governor, Murphy received 59 percent of the vote. He did not carry the state because of general disillusionment with the Democrat's New Deal policies, which may have been a more important factor.[36]

The automobile industry and the cause of labor flourished in Detroit for many years. However, during the 1950s, Detroit's domination of the industry began to weaken. The city lost over 100,000 manufacturing jobs as many businesses, such as Murray Auto Body, Packard, Hudson, and Studebaker, closed their Detroit operations. The scenario would be repeated by other companies in the years to come. Many workers and residents left the city. Corktown had been devoid of its Irish residents for many years. The Irish had departed it and other neighborhoods for the further edges of town and the suburbs.

Civil Rights and Public Service

By the 1960s African-Americans had inherited a city with a long history of discrimination in housing and employment, racial strife, and civic inaction. Theirs was a city where unemployment was double the national average. Confronting these problems in the firebrand 1960s was Detroit Democratic mayor Jerome Cavanaugh. In his first term, the Irish American mayor linked himself with the American Civil Rights Movement knowing that its mission was not confined to the South. In solidarity with Detroit's Rev. C. L. Franklin and Dr. Martin Luther King Jr., Cavanaugh walked down Woodward Avenue in Detroit's Great March for Freedom in 1963.

Cavanaugh had done more than march, an action that most mayors of his day would have avoided. His firm commitment to general civil rights was evidenced in many of his other deeds. In his first act as mayor, Cavanaugh ordered the abandonment of discriminatory hiring practices. He appointed African-Americans to several of his administrative posts and made social reformer George Edwards police commissioner. To generate revenue, Cavanaugh pushed Detroit's first income tax bill through Michigan's legislature. Through his work with President Johnson's War on Poverty, he sought to bring Model Cities dollars to Detroit. The Head of Detroit's NAACP in the mid-1960s said that although the Black community realized that Cavanaugh was not the Messiah, at least they now had a mayor who recognized that they were part of the city.[37]

The serious problems of Detroit, like those of other American inner cities, were more than any one man could fix. Government funds were continually cut. More importantly, Detroit continued to lose jobs as more factories and businesses left the city. Finally, many years of injustice exploded in flames on the streets of Detroit.

Exactly ten years before the rioting in Detroit, Fr. Solanus Casey died. He had been born in Wisconsin to immigrant Irish parents and named Bernard for his father. Upon entering the Capuchin Franciscan Order, he received the name Solanus. Fr. Casey soon came to Detroit where he spent his life working in service to the poor. During the Depression, he founded the Capuchin Soup Kitchen which still functions today. His death in July 1957 marked the end of a life dedicated to others. Pope John Paul II declared him venerable in 1995. Many expect him to become the first American-born male saint.[38]

Representing the state of Michigan in the U.S. Senate during most of the 1950s and 60s was Detroit's Patrick McNamara. Elected to that office in 1954 and again in 1960, the son of Irish immigrants had moved to Detroit from Massachusetts as a young man and made it his home. In so doing he had followed the path of so many of those early Irish immigrants who had made their way from the eastern states. And, like them, he had come to work. Arriving in 1921, he headed a construction crew. A pipe fitter, he became president of a local unit of the Pipe Fitters Union. Between 1939 and 1945 he served as vice-president of the Detroit Federation of Labor and went on to become the first president of the Auto Workers of America (AWA). The forerunner of the UAW, AWA was the Detroit Automobile industry's original industrial union. McNamara's leadership career culminated in his election as Michigan's democratic senator.[39] Detroit's Federal Building now bears his name.

Along the river rests another modern Detroit landmark named for a U.S. senator from Michigan. The Philip Hart Plaza is a reminder of the Irish American who served in the senate from 1959 until his death in office in 1976. A graduate of the University of Michigan's Law School, his Detroit law practice was interrupted when he fought in World War II. He was severely wounded during the D-Day assault in Normandy. While serving in Washington, he became known as the conscience of the senate. The Philip A. Hart Senate Office Building is testimony to the respect with which he was held by his colleagues.

A champion of liberal Democratic causes, President Johnson selected Hart to marshal the Voting Rights Act of 1965 through a southern filibuster. His work continued with the passage of the Open Housing-Civil Rights Act of 1968. Hart was a champion of consumer-related issues as well. It was he who sponsored and stood firmly behind the legislation that established Michigan's Sleeping Bear Dunes and Pictured Rocks as National Lakeshores. At his request, a memorial scholarship fund was established in his name at the Upper Peninsula's Lake Superior State University.

Detroit: A Strong Irish Presence

Irish immigrants no longer make their way to Detroit in great waves. However, their descendents, as well as the more recently arrived, provide a strong Irish presence. Though they live scattered throughout the area, the Detroit Irish are represented in more than twenty-five organizations. They come together in social, charitable, cultural, and political activity and fraternity.

Their Irish heritage is paid tribute in Detroit's annual St. Patrick's Day Parade sponsored by the United Irish Societies. The main route takes them down Michigan Avenue in Corktown "closer to Holy Trinity" than other routes would bring them.[40] It has been over 150 years since Holy Trinity's spirit came to rest there in the old Irish neighborhood. Much has changed yet Holy Trinity remains the embodiment of Irish ethnicity in Detroit.

Perhaps Holy Trinity is symbolic of all the churches scattered throughout the city which were so important to their Irish parishioners. St. Leo's, St. Cecilia's, St. Vincent's, Holy Redeemer, and St. Peter's Episcopal are among them. Detroit's parishes were of major importance to the ethnic Irish. Their lives centered around them as spiritual, educational, social, and recreational hubs. Where one grew up was designated by a parish, not a street name.

Ste. Anne's, the first church in which Detroit's Irish immigrants worshiped, remains a working parish though it is in its fifth building since 1701. It is the second oldest continuous Catholic parish in the United States, with St. Augustine's in Florida being the oldest. Located near the Ambassador Bridge, the Mother Church of the Northwest Territory, the first cathedral of the diocese of Detroit, remains a symbol of the French Catholic influence that made so many early Irish immigrants welcome in Detroit.

Holy Trinity is now mainly a Mexican-American parish. It has also served Detroit's Maltese community. Those who enter its doors today will see three plaques mounted on its wall—one to the Maltese, one to Mexican-Americans, and one to the Irish.

The Irish Beyond Detroit

Most people tend to think of Irish immigrants in the United States as urban settlers in the big eastern cities of New York, Philadelphia, and Boston. However, significant numbers of the Irish settled in rural areas of the Midwest from the plains of Nebraska and Iowa to the lumber camps of Wisconsin and the farmlands of Ohio, Illinois, Indiana, and Michigan. In Michigan we can find Irish settlers in every corner of the state. Wherever they settled they contributed to the growth and development of that area.

Often the most indelible mark of their presence was the establishment of a Catholic parish that was the center of their social, economic, and cultural life, just as it had been in Ireland. As previously noted, many of today's American Irish, especially those from urban areas, speak of where they grew up and identify themselves by their parish name, which often quickly locates them for other Irish.

Irish protestants also settled in rural areas but assimilated rapidly to American ways becoming indistinguishable from Anglo-Americans. In most instances they did not retain a sense of Irish ethnic identity. Furthermore, some Irish-born immigrants were not Irish but descendants of the English landlord class and did not personally identify themselves as Irish. In fact, many agreed with the Duke of Wellington, 31 himself of Irish birth, when he is alleged to have said "just because one is born in a stable doesn't make one a horse."

The Reverends Isaac McCoy and Peter Dougherty were early, Irish-born protestant missionaries to Michigan. McCoy left Pennsylvania for Michigan where in 1822 he worked among the Potawatomi Indians at Niles. He established a mission to the Ottawa Indians in the Grand River valley in 1824–25, but abandoned the operation after he lost control. Between 1835 and 1836 he unsuccessfully attempted to prevent the establishment of a Catholic mission in the Grand Rapids area.

Dougherty, who had fled Ulster to escape the penal laws, graduated from Princeton University and came to Michigan to work among the Ojibwa and Ottawa Indians. He established a Presbyterian missionary school and church in 1839 in the Leelanau Peninsula of northwest Michigan. The church still stands today near Omena just north of Suttons Bay. Dougherty later founded another mission church in Emmet County on Bear Creek again to serve the Ojibwa and Ottawa.

It would be imprudent to attempt an exhaustive discussion of all the small predominantly Irish communities that are distributed throughout Michigan. We have attempted to present a representative sample of Irish settlements in order to introduce the reader to the widespread presence of the Irish in the history of the Wolverine state.

The Irish of Beaver Island

The islands of northern Lake Michigan with their ample forest resources and plentiful fishing grounds offered an inviting environment for those from the west coast of Ireland. In the 1830s, Irish fishermen had established themselves on Mackinac Island and began exploring the rich waters surrounding it. By the late 1830s, they had ventured into the islands of the Beaver Archipelago and began to establish fishing camps, small settlements, and isolated households. Beaver is the largest of the ten islands located about thirty miles out in the lake from Charlevoix. It became a focal point for Irish settlement. Beaver Island was a beautiful place, covered with forests and cranberry marshes and punctuated by inland lakes.

Bonner Homestead, Beaver Island, circa 1895. Courtesy of Beaver Island Historical Society.

In 1845, Patrick Kilty, an Irish immigrant, participated in the government survey of Beaver in preparation for the sale of land. Kilty and his aunt and uncle, Ann and Patrick Luney, soon bought some of the island. However, the early Irish settlement was halted in 1847 when Mormons led by James Strang arrived. Under Strang, the Mormons gained control of the island, prospered, and established the settlement of St. James. They then proceeded to drive the non-Mormons off the island. By 1852 few non-Mormons were left on Beaver.

On June 16, 1856, two dissident Mormons shot and killed Strang. As soon as the news reached Mackinac Island, a group of armed men set sail for Beaver and attacked the leaderless community. With the help of the Coast Guard, the Mormons were driven off the island and most of the Irish exiles returned establishing new fishing camps and farms and occupying former Mormon sites. Black John Bonner, a Donegal man, was one of the first to reoccupy the island, while Patrick Luney became the St. James lighthouse keeper. A group of County Mayo men, the five Martin brothers, moved their families and their fishing business to the island. Beaver was on its way to becoming the Emerald Isle of Lake Michigan. According to Cashman, Beaver was at the center of the richest freshwater fishing in the world.[41] Between 1830 and 1890, the islanders harvested sturgeon, lake trout, perch, herring, and whitefish.

Beaver Island was covered with 55 acres of shipbuilding-quality hardwood.[42] Wood unsuitable for planking was used to fuel the lake steamers that regularly passed the island. At various times, islanders manufactured wooden fish boxes and extracted fish oil used in lubricating motors. Clearing the woods provided employment for many of the immigrants. After the land was cleared by the noted Irish brawn, it was cultivated yielding many good harvests of hay, potatoes, and oats and nurtured cattle, sheep, and poultry. Farming on Beaver was similar to that in Ireland with small plots that could be worked with basic implements, strong hands, and sturdy backs. The Irish could now labor for themselves, not for an English landlord.

Most of the Mackinac fisherman originally came from Aranmore, an island off the coast of County Donegal. The early Irish on Mackinac generally fished with gill nets catching huge quantities with a minimum of effort. When gill nets were replaced with pound nets, they were able to haul out fish at the rate of two to three tons per day.[43] However, this innovation depleted the fishery faster than nature could renew it. The decline in the size of fish schools resulted in job losses in fishing, net making, and boat building. Fishing remained important until the invasion of the sea lamprey, which seriously disrupted the traditional fishing economy of the island.

Later Irish immigrants looking for a better life came from New York City, the Pennsylvania coalfields, Toronto, Canada, and directly from Ireland. Those from New York left for Beaver to escape the squalid, crowded tenements, and slums as well as the rampant anti-Irish discrimination of Eastern cities. Pennsylvania miners wished to escape the oppressive work conditions of the dangerous mines and the vicious coercive tactics of the mine owners and their private armies.

The Canadian contribution to the Beaver Island Irish came from a large concentration of Irish settlement in Toronto. Many of them had originally emigrated from Aranmore. They may have heard about Beaver from Charlie O'Donnell who wrote his wife Grace in praise of an

McCann's Dock, Beaver Island with members of the Gallagher and McCann families and dog Rex in 1928. Courtesy of Beaver Island Historical Society.

island that reminded him of Aranmore.[44] This group included McCauleys, Boyles, Gallaghers, O'Donnells, Connaghams, and Mc-Donoughs, all of whom probably began arriving sometime in 1857 and were soon joined by other relatives.

The Irish who survived and fled the Great Starvation and eventually came to Beaver Island brought memories and stories of death by disease and starvation, and further stories of evictions and English oppression. They had survived horrors that none of us today could possibly imagine. According to Collar, the first large group of post-starvation arrivals initially settled in America's eastern urban areas before becoming aware of Beaver Island's possibilities.[45]

Families on Beaver began to save money to bring their relatives over from Ireland. Beaver Island became well known in Aranmore from letters and stories as a place where a poor man might be free. From the 1860s to 1884, immigrants continued to arrive largely from Donegal. The Irish on Beaver Island were elated to be in America, a country that had defeated the British. For example, Collar relates how July 4 was always a raucous holiday for the Irish who had endured centuries of brutal oppression, racism, and cultural genocide at the hands of the hated British empire.[46]

Throughout the island's history, its dominant religion has been Catholicism. In 1857, St. Ignatius, a log church, was built on the southeast end of the island two miles north of Cables Bay.[47] For about 10 years it served the needs of about 30 Irish immigrants. After its closure, the building was converted to a school. In 1860, Fr. Patrick Murray was sent by Bishop Baraga to Beaver and he proceeded to build the first part of the Holy Cross Church. It has been reported that the location of the church was a source of contention between those who wanted it in town and those who preferred an inland site. A compromise located the church a mile and half from St. James Harbor. Murray remained at Holy Cross until the spring of 1866. He was replaced by Fr. Peter Gallagher from Ireland, a fluent Gaelic speaker who continued to strengthen the parish and its role in the community. Gallagher remained at Holy Cross until his death on November 10, 1898.

The parish has been a hub of community activities throughout the years. Netting bees to make and repair fish nets were held in the parish hall as were many other social events. Even today those who have relocated in Chicago, Grand Rapids, and other places continue to support projects associated with the church. In November 1957, the 97-year-old church was moved into the town of St. James.

Many of the early Beaver Islanders spoke Gaelic. Some never learned English and Gaelic survived well into the twentieth century. An Irish system of nicknames was maintained to differentiate among different families and generations that had many similar names. Weddings and wakes on the island reminded one of Ireland. Sommers relates how the early Beaver Islanders were quite capable dancers with respect to both the solo step dances like jigs, reels, and hornpipes and set dancing.[48] Both were an important part of rural life-ways in Ireland. Using many of the life-ways transferred from Ireland to Beaver, the islanders remained pretty independent of the mainland until World War II.

Music and dance were the basic forms of entertainment on Beaver.[49] The island was referred to as "an Island of Fiddlers" and Allen Lomax and Ivan Walter came there to record Patrick Bonner, an old time fiddler. Many of the songs originated in Ireland such as "Leaving

St. James business district in 1937. Courtesy of Beaver Island Historical Society.

of Aranmore," but others were written by the settlers and their descendants. These songs reflect life on the island and include "Lost on Lake Michigan" and "The Gallant Tommy Boyle." Like Irish immigrants elsewhere, songs were used to remind them of the homeland and the troubles they had had to endure as well as their experiences in the new land. Music with Irish ethnic roots still flourishes on the island among the modern descendants of the pioneers. However, according to Sommers, the younger generation prefers contemporary music and not the old tunes.[50]

A strong pride in their Irish ethnicity still prevails on the island and among those who have left for other places. The Beaver Island Historical Society actively promotes the preservation of island history. St. Patrick's Day remains an important occasion for celebration. Irish place names such as McCauley's Bay, Kelty's Point, Donegal Bay, Conn Point, Green Bay, and others are prominent in the cultural geography of Beaver. Irish influences on architecture, fishing, and shipbuilding industries are evident still. The culture of Beaver Island today is greatly influenced by the historical adaptations of the original Irish culture in order to survive and prosper in the face of the unique circumstances of the island ecosystem. Out of a year round population today of 400, about 35 percent are of Irish descent.

The Irish in the Upper Peninsula

A copper boom in the Keewenau peninsula in the western part of Michigan's Upper Peninsula began in the 1840s. The mines attracted immigrant labor, including many Irish. According to Mulligan, the Great Starvation of the mid 1840s led to considerable migration to Michigan.[51] The immigrants worked the copper pits and underground mines as Michigan became a leading producer of American copper. According to O'Neil, by the end of the American Civil War the Keewenau peninsula produced three-quarters of the nation's copper.[52] By 1887, Michigan accounted for 87 percent of the nation's copper production, a supremacy it maintained until the rise of the copper mines of Butte, Montana.[53]

According to O'Neil, the majority of Irish copper miners in the Keewenau were from the Beara peninsula in West Cork, Ireland. O'Neil also notes that the four most common names in Houghton County, Michigan, were Sullivan, Harrington, Shea, and Murphy, which was the same case as in the Beara peninsula. Houghton County also had common names like Lynch, McCarthy, Dwyer, and Crowley just as one would find in the Beara peninsula. By 1870, the Irish were the largest single foreign-born group numbering 31.4 percent of the total foreign-born in the region.[54]

In the early years, Irish miners dominated the copper fields not just as laborers but as skilled miners. O'Neil suggests that the high numbers of skilled miners among the Irish was probably due to their experience in the copper mines in Cork.[55]

Rivalry between Irish and Cornish miners was common and is often dismissed as being due to religious bigotry between the Catholic Irish and Protestant Cornish. However, Todd views the rivalry as one of "skill envy" between unskilled Irish laborers and skilled Cornish miners.[56] O'Neil, on the other hand, proposes that competition for skilled jobs was the problem and that the Irish actually held more skilled jobs than the Cornish.[57] He further suggests that the origin of ethnic job competition could be traced to the copper mines of Ireland where the British had imported Cornish miners as bosses.

However, not all of the Irish in the copper country worked the mines. Many became teamsters loading ore. Others worked in mills that crushed and sorted the ore. Still others became small shopkeepers or tradesmen. By the 1870s, the Irish were serving as doctors, lawyers, merchants, and small business owners, such as saloonkeepers. They also became involved in local politics. In 1863, Edward Ryan from County Tipperary was elected Sheriff of Houghton County. He developed a reputation for even handed, unbiased enforcement of the law.[58] In Keewenau County, Patrick O'Brien from County Cork became a justice of the peace. He had been a miner in the local Cliff mine. At this time it would appear that the Irish were exhibiting significant social mobility in the copper country.

As in other geographic areas, the Catholic Church was an important institution for the Irish. Their communities often grew up around them. By 1859, according to Mulligan, five heavily Irish parishes existed in the copper country.[59] They were St. Ignatius in Houghton, Holy Redeemer in Eagle Harbor, Our Lady of the Assumption in Clifton, St. Mary's in Rockland, and St. Ann's (later St. Patrick's) in Hancock.

The Irish organized their own cultural and benevolent societies. By 1860, the St. Patrick's Society in Houghton had 70 members and by its incorporation in 1874, it had grown to 180. Other units existed throughout the region.[60] The Ancient Order of Hibernians (AOH) and the Robert Emmett Society were also present. St. Patrick's Day was a special occasion by the 1860s with dances and parades common. Between 1870 and 1884, AOH units existed in Escanaba, Norway, Quinnesec, Humboldt, Negaunee, Marquette, Ishpeming, Hancock, Calumet, and Iron Mountain. By 1894, the number of AOH units in the Upper Peninsula outnumbered those in the Lower Peninsula by 9 to 4.[61] In 1896, an AOH convention was held in Escanaba. AOH membership tended to be heavy among miners, just as in Molly Maguire country in eastern Pennsylvania.

Irish nationalist groups were also prominent in the 1860s. The Fenian Brotherhood was active throughout the copper region. The local Irish contributed and supported their militant campaign to free Ireland from British rule. It would also appear that the Clan Na Gael, a secret society founded in 1867 after the demise of the Fenians, was present under the guise of the Robert Emmett Society. Later, according to Thurner, during the first six months of 1921, Houghton County sent $6,000 to Ireland for relief at the conclusion of the Anglo-Irish War of Independence.[62]

The Irish presence in the copper country inspired the typical anti–Irish Catholic prejudice. Local newspapers such as the *Mining Gazette* were usually very critical of the Irish and their activities. According to Mulligan, it was common practice when reporting criminal and perceived anti-social behavior to identity the ethnicity if the individual involved was Irish.[63] In the Irish conflicts with Cornish mine bosses, the local papers tended to side with the bosses.

By the 1890s, Irish miners were a significant part of the workforce and many other Irish were important contributors to the community life of many towns. However, by the 1920s they had virtually disappeared from the copper country. Only cultural remnants, such as Irish Hollow cemetery near the abandoned Minesota Mine in Rockland, Ontonagon County, physically remain as evidence of their once prominent presence. O'Neil suggests that the majority of second generation Michigan-born American Irish miners migrated to the Montana copper region near Butte accompanied by their aging parents, thus accounting for the diminished Irish presence.[64]

The copper country was not the only area of the Upper Peninsula settled by the Irish. Some came to the Marquette Iron Range to work as miners or blacksmiths and blast furnace workers. However, the Irish were not as numerous as Cornish miners in the iron range. Of course some Irish arrived to work the lumber camps as lumberjacks.

At the eastern end of the Upper Peninsula, many Irish immigrants came to work on the St. Mary's Falls Ship Canal that would connect Lake Superior with Lake Huron. The canal was needed to eliminate the arduous task of unloading ore at Sault Ste. Marie onto tram cars that carried it to waiting ships on Lake Huron, which in turn would transport the ore to mills in Ohio and Pennsylvania.[65] Work on the canal commenced in June 1853. According to Dickinson, sick and starved

Irish immigrants, half of whom weighed less then 100 pounds, died in the thousands while working on this canal.[66] Canal work in this part of Michigan was harsh, with subzero temperatures in the winter and murderous swarms of black flies and mosquitoes in the summer and early fall. In 1854, a cholera epidemic killed hundreds of workers. When the canal was finished in April 1855, it was a physical marvel at 5,700 feet long, 13 feet deep, and an average of 85 feet wide.[67] The canal was the result of brute physical labor and the death and maiming of many laborers. Many of the survivors settled in the surrounding towns and on rural farmsteads.

Eastern Michigan

In 1823, the first Irish families began to settle in Northfield Township, Washtenaw County. They were farmers who began tilling the rich farmland of southeastern Michigan. Between 1829 and 1831, they established the first English speaking Catholic parish in Michigan. The original parish consisted of 15 Irish families. The family names included obviously Irish ones like Keenan, McKernan, Sullivan, McIntyre, Neligan, Walsh, Donovan, Galligan, and Purtell. In 1831 they built the first public building in the township, a log chapel. The parish became the center of the community's social life.

Northfield Township was an area that included several lakes, marshes, and forestland. Wild game to supplement the diet was abundant, including turkey, deer, quail, partridge, and ducks. Wild honey was also harvested and fishing was excellent. The wild marsh grasses were harvested and fed to cattle in the winter. Wolves often posed a problem for livestock such as cattle and sheep. The staple diet for farm families included bread, potatoes, corn, and salt pork. Cranberries and pumpkins were used for sauce and sassafras and sage tea were common local concoctions.

In 1837 the log chapel was torn down and replaced. By 1850, the parish grew to 90 members necessitating its expansion. The church was named St. Bridget's, but by 1877 a new church was constructed and renamed St. Patrick's. According to a local story, competition was promoted between the Irish and Germans to select a new name. The group that gave the most money would select the name; St. Patrick's by the Irish or St. Joseph by the Germans. However, it is said that the Irish won because the Irish wives of German farmers in typical Irish fashion controlled the family money and so it was contributed to the Irish side.[68]

Over the years, one of the important social activities was a wood cutting bee in which each family cut one cord of wood per year for the church. It is probable the first parish organization, "The Men's Club," grew out of this activity. In the 1870s, Patrick Purtell, a second generation Irish American, founded the first formal society *The St. Patrick's Temperance and Benevolent Society* as an educational, charitable, and social organization. The organization produced a play written and directed by Purtell, "Whiskey Demon," but local farmers were not as moved by it as middle class moralists would have liked.[69] The gatherings after Sunday Mass were important social occasions for the whole community. As in other areas of the Great Lakes, German and Irish farmers got on well and frequently intermarried, but the Irish Catholics tended to avoid the Protestants in nearby Whitmore. Eventually the Northfield Irish looked to the Ann Arbor Irish community for friends and fellow travelers.

As in other areas of the country, the Irish seemed to gravitate toward local politics. Michael Patrick Stubbs came to Northfield in 1825–26 and helped to recruit the first dozen or so Irish families. He became a leading advocate for the Irish community. He was elected in 1835 to represent Washtenaw County at the constitutional convention for the new state of Michigan. Stubbs also served on the assembly that ratified the compromise that gave the Toledo area to Ohio. He was active in promoting the election of anti-mason candidates in local politics. The masons were an anti-Catholic group and thus were disliked heartily by the Irish. Patrick Wall, born in Ireland in 1824, was elected constable as well as Northfield Township supervisor. William H. McIntyre, whose father and wife were born in Ireland, became a constable in Northfield and later moved to Ann Arbor where he operated a grocery and served as a deputy sheriff. Pat McKernan from Northfield became a lawyer in Ann Arbor and served both as a justice of the peace and a circuit court commissioner.

The second generation Irish were active in the area of education. Many a young person from the community entered the field of education. Education was highly encouraged for their offspring by the less educated older Irish.

Of course the priest played an important role in every Irish community. The Irish preferred to have their own as priests, especially in the early years. Fr. Patrick Kelly from Ireland followed Irish immigrants into Michigan in 1829. After a brief stay in Detroit, he moved to the Ann Arbor area, where for six years he roamed southern Michigan as far west as Marshall. In 1831 he settled in Northfield and was revered by the Irish community. The Irish of Northfield were very upset when he was sent to minister to Irish immigrants in Milwaukee, Wisconsin. Kelly returned to the region in 1843 to minister in Livingstone and Oakland Counties. He established his headquarters at Green Oaks St. Patrick's, but it is a mystery why. Pinckney in Putnam Township had far more Irish than Green Oaks. However, Kelly maintained his close ties to Northfield.

Another Irish priest, Fr. Thomas Cullen, was in residence in the area between 1839 and 1864. It was Cullen who established a mission parish at St. Patrick's at Green Oaks. After Fr. Kelly returned, Cullen left the township and proceeded to establish St. Thomas Church in Ann Arbor in 1843. Originally masses were held in the homes of parishioners, all of whom had Irish names, such as the James Harrigans in Ann Arbor, the Peter Cowans in Dixboro, the John Condons in Freedom, and the Patrick Laveys in Dexter.[70] He also ministered to Irish settlements in Jackson and Marshall. In 1839, Cullen also established a largely Irish church, St. John's, in Ypsilanti. Both of these tough pioneer priests were very independent and set their own agendas. Like other Irish-born priests, they both tended to ignore the orders of their French bishops who complained to Rome about the quality of the Irish-born priests. It became a nationally contentious situation. Bishop England of Charleston, South Carolina, suggested the founding of American Seminaries in order to train an American-born clergy.

St. Thomas' was founded to serve the growing Irish community in Ann Arbor. Fr. Cullen also built churches in Dexter (1846), Jackson (1846), and Marshall (1851). The arrival of The Michigan Central Railroad in the area brought Irish railroad workers and later a large number of Irish settlers. The Michigan Central reached Jackson in 1844, Marshall in early 1845, Battle Creek in November 1845, and Kalamazoo in February 1846.[71]

The Ann Arbor Irish community experienced continuous growth and remained a powerful element until after World War I. The town spawned many notable Irish lawyers, doctors, business people, and politicians. James S. Gorman, born in 1850, was a lawyer who graduated from the University of Michigan and became a democratic member of congress. Gorman's parents were from County Down and his grandfather, Edward Gorman, was imprisoned by the British for his part in the Irish Rebellion of 1798. John W. Dwyer, whose father came from Ireland, became a prominent lawyer as did Martin Cavanaugh whose parents also were born in Ireland. Cavanaugh also became president of the local board of education. James Henry O'Toole was a doctor of dentistry whose father owned hardware and sewing machine businesses in Ann Arbor. Finally, John O'Hara was born in Ann Arbor on May 1, 1888, while his father John was attending law school at the University of Michigan.[72] O'Hara became a priest, eventually the president of the University of Notre Dame, a bishop, and finally a cardinal.

In 1843, Ann Arbor's Irish Repeal Association was formed by Fr. Cullen to help people in Ireland who sought to bring about the end of their union with England.[73] In the spring of 1847, Fr. Cullen and a committee that consisted of William O'Hara, Daniel McIntyre, and Patrick Kelly organized relief efforts on behalf of the people suffering during the Great Starvation.[74] In the 1880s, the Irish National League had annual St. Patrick's banquets to raise funds for the struggling people of Ireland.[75] St. Patrick's Day was also observed by topical speeches concerning Robert Emmett (the Irish patriot executed by the English in 1803 for rebellion), the Irish in America, and the struggle for Irish freedom. A play by Joseph Clarke, "Robert Emmett," was performed.

Irish settlements were established in other parts of the Northfield/Ann Arbor area. In 1843 in Deerfield Township, Livingstone County, thir-

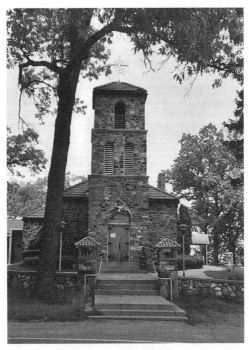

St. Joseph's Shrine in the Irish Hills near Brooklyn in rural Lenawee County was founded by 20 Irish settlers in 1845. Photo by S. P. Metress.

teen Irish immigrant families, mostly from County Longford, founded the Catholic church St. Peter and Paul which was renamed St. Augustine's in 1870. This church served Irish settlers in Deerfield and nearby Tyrone Township. It is said that the original Irish settlers walked from New York State, encouraged by the availability of good farmland at $3 an acre.

Refugees from the Great Starvation settled in Lenawee County in the 1840s. They built St. Joseph's Catholic Church at Cambridge Center near the present village of Brooklyn.

Others of them settled in the rich farming area near Hudson, Michigan, in Lenawee County. The nearby hills reminded many of Ireland. The early family names included Dwyer, Dougherty, Rooney, Delany, Dillon, Haley, O'Reilly, Monahan, and Moriarty, some of which are still on the parish roles at Sacred Heart Catholic Church in Hudson.

The first masses were held in farm houses. The people eventually built a small frame church in Medina Township in an area referred to as "Catholic Hill." In 1858, the parish was relocated to Hudson and named Sacred Heart. St. Mary's of Good Counsel parish in Adrian was founded in the early 1840s by Irish people bearing names like Nelly, Carey, Hayes, Rice, and Murphy.

In Shiawasee County, Irish immigrants moved to Owosso in 1840 and by 1847 had built the first log church, St. Paul's. Catholic Irish railroaders added to the Irish element in Owosso. West Owosso was the home of the Cavanaugh brothers who entered the catholic priesthood. Fr. John J. Cavanaugh, CSC served as the president of the University of Notre Dame from 1946 to 1952, while Fr. Francis Cavanaugh, CSC became the Dean of Arts and Letters there. Irish farmers and lumbermen settled in the Midland, Auburn, and Freeland areas where they founded St. Brigid's Catholic Church with help from the famous Dow family.

Saginaw, Bay City, Flint, Alpena, and Port Huron had small Irish settlements. The Irish settled around St. Joseph's and St. Mary's parish in East Saginaw and St. Andrew's in West Saginaw. In Bay City, they clustered around St. James, while in Alpena their parish was St. Bernard's. The Saginaw/Bay City area was settled by significant numbers of Irish immigrants lured by commercial fishing, lumbering, and labor. Irish laborers entered the area to work on the Saginaw and Grand Canal that was to link Lakes Michigan and Huron as well as on the new Territorial Road. The canal was never completed but many of the workers settled down in the area. Saginaw developed as a major timber port and the Irish took to the woods as lumberjacks. As early as the 1820s, Irish fishermen came to Saginaw, Bay City, and Alpena in search of whitefish. In Saginaw, Timothy Tarsney, born of Irish immigrants in Hillsdale County, came to lead the Democratic political machine that controlled the Saginaw Valley in the late 1800s. He graduated from the University of Michigan law school in 1872 and served as the city attorney of what was then called East Saginaw. He also served two terms in the United States House of Representatives.

In 1855, the first pioneers of Irish ancestry came to Seville Township in Gratiot County and settled an area that came to be known as Irishtown. The early Irish family names included Connelly, Murray,

Battle, McLaughlin, Egan, and Manion. Other Irish families settled in nearby Summer, Lincoln, and Coe townships. The settlers obtained their land through the Graduation Act that allowed a man to acquire land by paying 50¢ an acre and living on the land for 18 months.[76] The land around Irishtown was composed of wild barren swamps and oak forests. Irish farmers and lumbermen turned the land into the viable farms that came to characterize the area. In 1868, they founded St. Patrick's church as a mission station of Hubbardston.

In the early years, the Irish emigrants had to travel over 50 miles to Ionia for mass. The first church in Irishtown, a log building, was erected in 1868. The building committee was comprised entirely of Irishmen. The church remained a mission station of varied affiliations for many years. A permanent brick church was erected by Fr. Francis B. Brogger, between 1897 and 1900, with the aid of his flock.

Western Michigan

The first Irish to come to the Grand Rapids area arrived by stagecoach in 1835. They came to build the canal around the rapids of the Grand River and a wing dam. The Irish sang as they worked with their two wheeled dump carts, wheelbarrows, picks, and shovels. However, when the skeletons of local Indian mounds appeared, the Irish refused to dig. They also built a flourmill and the foundation for a sawmill and worked on the harbor. By 1841 more Irish began to arrive and by 1846 a distinct Irish settlement had been established.[77] The Irish "shantytown" was located at the foot of the rapids, where the boats docked on south Monroe Ave.[78] In fact, they were strong enough to contribute money to the relief fund for victims of the Great Starvation. By the 1860s, the Irish of this area were in a position to support the Fenian revolutionary movement.

Irish women generally worked as domestics while the men worked the salt works and gypsum mines. Irish stonemasons and sawmill work-ers were common. Steamers coming up the Grand River from Lake Michigan had crews that were heavily Irish. Many Irish gradually moved out of the "shantytowns" near the mills, mines, and railroad yards to other areas around Grand Rapids.

The Ancient Order of Hibernians was established in Grand Rapids in 1883. The Kent County division No. 1 became the largest and most active in Michigan. They initially met on Canal Street and later constructed the Hibernian Hall in 1889, on Ottawa NW. A ladies auxiliary was established in 1894 and a band in 1907. The band was prominent in the annual celebration of Daniel O'Connell's birthday on August 6th, as well as on St. Patrick's Day. At one time, the Grand Rapids' AOH was the second largest in the United States, with only New York surpassing it.[79]

St. Andrew's parish, established in 1854, became a largely Irish church. By 1858, it had added a Catholic school. In the early years, the priest from St. Andrew's had to circuit ride to minister to Irish Catholic enclaves in Ludington and Ionia. The Parish built a center for rallies, plays, and concerts. Luce Hall was the envy of the area. By 1870, St. Andrew's had 4,000 parishioners who were mostly Irish.[80] St. James's, founded in 1870 to serve West Talmadge and Walker townships, was largely Irish. In 1873, the Sisters of Mercy, under Mother Joseph Lynch, were brought to Grand Rapids to teach by Fr. Patrick McManus from County Longford.

Fr. McManus, who served 1872–1885, was an energetic advocate for the Irish community. In 1888, John Clancy a pioneer Irish lumberman and wholesale grocer in Grand Rapids left $60,000 plus a farm to build an orphanage.[81] St. John's Home was completed in 1899.

The area around Grand Rapids saw early Irish settlement. In 1839, the first Irish families to purchase land north of the Grand River were the Devines, Fords, and Soules. They were followed in 1843 by the Byrnes, McCarthys, Sullivans, Kennedys, Farrells, and Giles. Many more Irish came into the area after they were offered land by the government as payment for their work on the Indiana Railroad.

An Irish settlement first called Cannonsburg, then Grattan, and later Parnell was established in 1844. It was a crossroads center for Irish settlers in Grattan, Vergennes, Cannon, Ada, and Oakfield townships. Fr. James Crumley christened the settlement Parnell, a befitting postmark, when their post office was established at Bresnahans Store. This area remained almost completely Irish for many years.

A church-planning committee was formed in 1844. It consisted of Richard Giles, William Byrne, Michael Farrell and Dennis McCarthy.

Aerial view of Parnell and St. Patrick's Church in the 1950s, showing St. Patrick's church, rectory, school, and cemetery, as well as Bresnahan's Store and Heffernan's Mercantile. Courtesy of Pat Nugent, St. Patrick's Parish historian (via Eileen Verlin).

The next year, St. Patrick's was built on land donated by Richard Giles.[82] To accommodate its growing congregation a new church was built in 1859 on land donated by John Sullivan. In 1860 St. Patrick's had a predominately Irish congregation numbering 1,000.[83] The church burned and was rebuilt in 1868. Another fire reclaimed it necessitating yet another rebuilding in 1876. Fr. Crumley started the first school in 1892. St. Patrick's Church became the center piece of community activity for many years. In the 1840s it began to become famous for its annual supper on or about August 15th, the Feast of the Assumption of Mary.[84] Even today, the area remains aware of and connected to its Irish roots.

In 1852, St. Mary's of Berlin, later changed to Marne, located 10 miles west of Grand Rapids in Ottawa County, was established. Irish settlers had come to the area in 1843.[85] The first mass was held in 1845 at the cabin of an Irishman named Patrick Pendergast.

South and east of Grand Rapids in Cascade township, Edward Lennon from Wicklow, Ireland by way of Quebec purchased 80 acres of land in 1836.[86] The first mass was held in 1849 in Lennon's cabin and by 1856, 47 Irish catholic families were settled in the township. The early families had names like McKnight, Lennon, Madigan, Shay, Nulty, Sheehan, Riordan, Flannery, Henessey, and Burn. St. Mary's church was erected in 1856 and was replaced by a new church in 1859. In 1866, the parish of St. Patrick's in Bowne was founded. Original family names included Flynn, O'Reilly, O'Hara, Gougherty, McGinnis, O'Connor, Hoey, Farrell, McGary, and McCullough. The Bernard Flynn House was the site of the early masses, but the parish never had a resident pastor.[87]

In the Grand Rapids area, not all residents accepted the growing influence of the Catholic Church. In the 1920s, Fr. Dennis Malone of St. Andrew's had to take on the KKK as it and its allies unsuccessfully tried to force all children to attend public school.

Irish culture and knowledge of one's Irish roots still flourish in the Grand Rapids area. The Ancient Order of Hibernians is still very active. Irish language and Irish dance classes are taught locally and several pubs offer Irish entertainment. The West Michigan Irish Festival is an annual summertime event held in nearby Muskegon.

Hubbardston in Ionia County is another area in which Irish immigrants settled. In 1849, John Cowman established a home in North Plains township. He later assisted the Welchs, Cusacks, Beahans, McKennas, Roaches, and Hogans in building and establishing farmsteads in the area. It was in his cabin that the Irish first attended mass and on his farm that they eventually built a little chapel. There they observed mass and participated in other devotions such as the Rosary.[88]

The influx of Irish settlers was so great that a new church was needed. In 1868 a new church that would accommodate over 400 persons was built on a hill overlooking the village of the Hubbardston. It was named St. John the Baptist. To the early Irish farmers, their church was their rock in the face of hunger, cold, and other vagaries of nature. It also was a refuge from prejudice and hostility. It was also the social and economic linchpin of the Irish community.

In the late 1870s, Irish immigrant families arrived in Portland, Ionia County. Their names were Moriarty, Matthews, Lawless, Kilmartin, and Manning. They worked in the lumber industry, farmed, and later served as railroaders. In 1878, they helped to build St. Patrick's Catholic Church to serve their spiritual needs.

In other parts of western Michigan, scattered Irish settlements and individuals made their mark. Wexford County was settled in 1870 by Irish immigrants, many of whom worked in the lumber industry. Irish heritage remains important even today in Manton where the townsfolk annually celebrate Irish Spring Days. Irish railroaders settled in Niles, while Irish sheep farmers were found in Cass County as early as the 1840s. In Whitehall, Michigan, Jerry Sullivan, the son of Irish immigrants to Illinois, worked in a shingle mill from age 11. By age 28, he was a half owner of the Cedar Michigan Shingle Mill and by 1903 owned a sawmill employing over 150 people.[89] Both Van Buren and Allegan Counties had small rural Irish settlements, while St. Joseph and Kalamazoo had significant populations with Irish heritage. Jim Dempsey emigrated in the midst of the Great Starvation and moved to Manistee after first settling in Pennsylvania. He worked as an axe man in the lumber camps and by 1875 co-owned the Manistee Lumber Company. He later owned the Manistee Tugline as well as serving the town as both Mayor and postmaster.[90]

The descendents of the Irish who settled and developed rural Michigan still live in many of the areas where their ancestors labored and died. In areas now urban, suburban, and rural, they celebrate their Irish heritage, learn their ancient language, form Irish organizations, and thrill to songs of old Ireland. Many seek to trace their Irish roots and travel to the land of their ancestors in search of deeper meaning or simply for a sense of adventure and curiosity.

Beyond the Neighborhood Today

United States history has always stressed the importance of prestigious individuals and institutions. It has told the stories of elites, not ethnics or immigrants. The size of the United States and the socioeconomic mobility of its population have worked against the maintenance of family, local, and ethnic ties. Geographic mobility has often separated the younger generation from their roots and from those who knew the most about their heritage.

Today, few live as part of a territorial ethnic group because of changing demographics and economic opportunities. However, to many, ethnicity remains important. Among the American-Irish, ethnicity has been preserved often by strong family memories spilling forth a plethora of stories intertwining family and Irish history. Membership in national ethnic organizations, such as the Ancient Order of Hibernians, Clan Na Gael, and the Friendly Sons of St. Patrick, has played an important part. Furthermore, many belong to local Irish organizations and cultural centers. The widespread existence of such national and local groups allows one to find Irish fraternity even in today's mobile society.

A great number of individuals attend or participate in Irish cultural activities, such as festivals, dances, sporting events, and Irish language and music classes. As always, the American-Irish press is influential with many subscribing to weekly and monthly papers, including *The Irish Echo, The Irish Edition* (Philadelphia), and *The Irish Herald* (San Francisco) or to magazines such as *Irish-America* or *Eire-Ireland*. The *Irish People Newspaper* helps one to keep up with the politics of British-occupied Ireland. Michigan is served by a monthly publication, *The Irish Connection*, which reports on Irish activities in Michigan with an emphasis on Detroit as well as news from Ireland.

Recently, there has been a great deal of interest among Americans about their Irish roots. Thus, many are doing genealogical studies and taking trips to Ireland in search of information about their families. Some go simply to enjoy the land of their ancestors.

Many have come to understand the horrific history of English oppression in Ireland and the stubborn resistance of the Irish people. Such knowledge has led a significant number of Irish-Americans to get involved in the present struggle in British occupied Ireland. They have joined and supported organizations like Irish Northern Aid, the Irish American Unity Conference, the Clan Na Gael, and Doors of Hope. They have participated in street protests, written letters to the media, and pressured political leaders. Indeed, Irish Nationalism still exists in America and will probably continue until the institutionalized discrimination and state violence of the northern counties ends with Ireland free and united.

Beyond Countyism to Nationalism

Irish-Americans have a long history of involvement in the struggle for Irish Freedom. The nature of their involvement and the reasons for it have varied over time. Irish American nationalism forced the Irish, regardless of their local Irish origins, to assume a larger Irish identity. As Patrick Ford, editor of the *Irish World*, once said, America led the Irish from the "littleness of countyism into a broad feeling of nationalism." Many Irish in America interpreted their ability to get ahead socio-economically as evidence that poverty, starvation, and oppression in Ireland was not their own fault. Rather, they were conditions imposed upon them by English colonialism. Irish-American economic advancement and rising political clout encouraged many to commit themselves to the struggle against English rule back home in Ireland.

In Michigan, organized participation dates back to the repeal movement of the 1840s, which sought to dissolve the political union of Britain and Ireland. Led by Daniel O'Connell in Ireland, the movement found support in America where a chapter of the Irish Repeal Association was founded in Detroit and elsewhere in Michigan in 1842. In 1858, Irish-Americans moved toward a more militant approach with the founding of the Fenian Brotherhood. This brotherhood was a secret society committed to the establishment of a free Republic of Ireland by the only means they thought possible, physical force. Many Irish-Michiganders joined the Union army during the American Civil War in order to train for their eventual fight for Irish freedom. The union army had over 50,000 Fenians in its ranks. After the war, a faction of the Fenians unsuccessfully invaded Canada. In June 1866, a large concentration of Fenians in Detroit forced the British to move 2,000 troops to the Michigan border at Windsor, Ontario, Canada. To raise funds for Fenian activities, Fenian Bonds were openly sold throughout Michigan in denominations from $10 to $100.

When the Fenians disbanded after military failure, they were succeeded by the Clan Na Gael. Founded in 1867, the Clan Na Gael advocated the military destruction of British rule in Ireland and quickly became an effective and influential political and fundraising force. In Detroit, it was headed for a time by Bishop Michael Gallagher. Gallagher's archives include a telegram from the Irish Republican Brotherhood in Dublin reporting the commencement of the Easter Rising of 1916. The Clan Na Gael, which provided at least $10,000 for the purchase of guns, was the only group in America to know about the Rising before it occurred.

The Clan Na Gael also cooperated in the founding of Ireland's National Land League with the goal of ending landlordism in Ireland. The Irish National Land and Industrial League was formed in the U.S. with various branches in Michigan. Its purpose was to raise money in funding the Land War in Ireland. Between 1879 and 1880, half a million Americans joined the League. The Clan Na Gael coordinated the American speaking tour of Charles Parnell, leader of the Land League.

Parnell visited major centers of Irish settlement across the United States, making stops in Michigan. The Land League Era represented an interesting combination of physical force and constitutional republicanism.

In 1918, the Clan Na Gael founded a front group, the Friends of Irish Freedom (FOIF), which became active in Michigan that same year. The Michigan Irish raised funds and public consciousness in support of the Irish Republican Army throughout the Anglo-Irish War of Independence. Bishop Gallagher was elected FOIF's second president. Gallagher was an outspoken advocate of Irish freedom. In 1921, when criticized by the *Detroit Free Press*, he referred to that paper as "the Detroit edition of the London Times."

Ireland was partitioned into two units by the British in 1921 at the conclusion of the Anglo-Irish War of Independence. Michigan, along with most of America, then became relatively quiet with respect to Irish freedom. However, as the nonviolent Northern Ireland civil rights movement of the late 1960s was crushed by loyalist violence and British intransigence, Irish republicanism once again rose from the ashes. Since partition, a small but constant migration of Irish Catholics out of Northeast Ireland had continued to bring news of the deprived state of living for nationalists in the six counties. Some of these immigrants formed a core group for the organization of Irish-American nationalist groups. In Detroit, a branch of the national Irish Northern Aid Committee was founded in 1971 by Joe Myles, Jimmy Doran, Mike McGann, and Tom McCauley. The unit grew rapidly after the Bloody Sunday Massacre in Derry, Ireland on January 30, 1972, where the British Army deliberately shot dead 14 unarmed civilians during a civil rights march.

Fundraising and political house parties started in Detroit in 1972. Eventually by 1974 such activities had to move to larger halls in order to accommodate the growing numbers of supporters. A constant stream of speakers came through Detroit ranging from Bernedette Devlin at Cobo Hall in 1972 to Gerry Adams of Sinn Fein at the Gaelic League in 1994, as well as other representatives of the Republican movement. Such events led to much press coverage, political education of the public, and generous fundraising.

Irish Northern Aid Committee marches in the Detroit St. Patrick's Day Parade in the mid-1980s, Led by Jim Phelan (center), a former Detroit Noraid president. Courtesy of Detroit INA.

In the period leading up to the 1981 Irish Hunger Strike political activity heightened and regular pickets were held at the British Consulate. Upon the death of hunger striker Bobby Sands in May 1981, a public march and memorial Mass were held at Holy Trinity Church. A 21-day sympathetic hunger strike by local Irish-Americans Mike Melody, who took only water, and Jennifer Miller, who consumed only liquids, was held at Holy Trinity. The year 1981 was a watershed in Irish history as Irish republican prisoners of war attempted to use the only weapon available to them, their own bodies through the hunger strike, to oppose British rule in Ireland. The Michigan Irish, along with other Americans, were morally energized by the courage of the prisoners and responded with intense political pressure. At one point during the 1981 hunger strike, they succeeded in getting the Michigan legislature to issue a notice stating that the British consulate was not welcome in Detroit. The consulate office was eventually closed in large part due to pressure from Irish-Americans.

The Irish American Unity Conference (IAUC), founded in 1981 by a Texas millionaire, focused on political lobbying in the United States. By 1985, a Detroit unit of this organization was operative. One of its most intense campaigns was the attempt to get state legislatures to enact into law the McBride Principles. These principles were aimed at preventing American companies from participating in anti-Catholic hiring practices in Northeast Ireland, as well as from doing business with companies that allowed such practices. The McBride Principles were passed by the Michigan legislature in February 1988. Led by the late Daniel O'Kennedy, the IAUC formed the Irish Information Service (IIS) to provide alternative sources on the situation in Northeast Ireland. For many years the Detroit chapter has literally underwritten the funding of the national office of the IAUC.

Irish nationalism in the United States has been closely linked with the labor movement in which Irish-Americans were among the earliest organizers and leaders. In Detroit, men like Pat Quinn, Pat Rice, Hugh Thompson, and Mike McGee, who helped build the United Auto Workers (UAW) into one of the most powerful unions in the United States, were staunch Irish nationalists. Union support for the Irish struggle has been strong throughout United States history and many Irish-American labor leaders have been outspoken in their support of Irish freedom.

Irish American political activists today are hard-nosed, combative, well informed, and dedicated. They are a self-confident group that has survived character assassination, unfounded ridicule, and government harassment. Many are aware of the parallels between Northeast Ireland and other trouble spots around the world and have reached out to other groups who struggle for justice. A great many have some experience in the six counties due to fact-finding tours and visits to friends and relatives. They are not romantic, sectarian, bogtrotters as some have attempted to portray them.

Surveying Irish America: Beyond Stereotypes

In the 1990 U.S. Census, over 40,000,000 people identified themselves as being of Irish ancestry. Thus, self-identification is massive. Moreover, more Protestants than Catholics identified as Irish. In reality, levels of ethnic identification are quite variable ranging from the once a year "green beer" or "St. Patrick's Day" Irish to those whose lives richly reflect their ethnic heritage. Regional variation in the intensity of ethnic identity and its expression also exists. The latter is largely related to the disparate nature of communities. Some have the numbers and/or the activities that provide opportunities to excite and energize as well as to exhibit Irish ethnicity.

Even today, old time structures and values are discernible among Irish-American families. Mothers are the strongest and most influential figures in these families, as they have been for generations. Contrary to the belief of many outsiders, they wield power and are rarely subordinate to their husbands. Mothers often control family finances and are the major decision makers. Family loyalty is intense. Siblings visit, help each other, and often feel anxious if relationships are strained. Extended family gatherings are still common and the significance of the Irish wake, though its nature has changed, has not diminished.

Higher education is valued for its utility in securing a job, not for its intrinsic value. In keeping with this point, Irish-Americans often pursue careers in pragmatic professions such as medicine, law, and teaching over those in esoteric ones such as art or philosophy. Economic welfare is an important issue, with thrift and saving greatly emphasized. Home ownership remains an important symbol of socioeconomic advancement.

Marriage outside the group is common with two-thirds reporting some mixed ancestry, German/Irish being the most frequent. The Irish-Americans have the largest families among European-ethnics. According to national surveys, Irish-American females expect to have more children than do their male counterparts, a reversal of the national picture. In contrast to earlier times, fewer individuals of both genders choose to remain single. Likewise, marriage is occurring on average at an earlier age today for both males (24.5 years old compared to their previous average of 34 years old) and females (22 years old compared to a their previous 31 years old).[91]

In spite of stereotypes that the Irish-Ameircans are ultraconservatives, National Opinion Research Center (NORC) data from the University of Chicago indicates a different picture. With the exception of Jews, Irish-Americans are the most likely of all American ethnic groups to be pro-feminist, indicating that they reject the idea that a woman's place is in the home; they approve of females having careers; and they would vote for a female president. According to the NORC, they also display little difference in gender-based support for feminism, unlike African-Americans and Jews among whom only females are most likely to support feminism. There seems to be no hard evidence for alleged sexual repression. Irish-Americans exhibit no differences from the national averages regarding marital, pre-marital, and extra-marital sex. Further, they are 13 percent less likely to condemn homosexuality than are other ethnic groups.[92]

Irish-Americans, according to the McGoldrick et al., have a tendency to deny pain while continuing to work. They wait longer before they see a doctor. It seems that pain as a sign of illness is less important than is its effects on work and appearance.[93]

Greeley's work seems to indicate that although many Irish drink, their related problems are no worse than among urban English-American Protestants and are less than among the Poles, Slovaks, and African-Americans. It is unfortunate that some link drinking with their identity, perpetuating societal stereotypes.

A higher percentage of Irish Catholics, with the exception Jews, send their children to college compared with other ethnic groups. Many Irish came through the parochial school system built by their ancestors, which was often branded inferior and clannish by biased White Anglo-Saxon Protestants. However, parochial students surveyed in Greeley's research were not more clannish and actually performed more liberally on social issues than did their public school counterparts.[94] These same parochial schools are a modern day refuge from the poor quality and chaos of many urban public schools, especially for minorities in the inner city. Today, parochial school graduates go on to elite non-Catholic universities, as well as to the University of Notre Dame, Boston College, Fordham University, and Georgetown University.

Beyond the Neighborhood

That Irish-Americans still worry about what the neighbors think may be an artifact of the virulent anti-Irish nativism of earlier times when they were not welcome in many communities and social circles. To

Heinzman School of Irish Dance performing in Detroit.

many, embarrassing one's family in view of outsiders remains a serious social concern. This factor has possibly affected the involvement of many in the modern Irish nationalist struggles, which the American media has demonized. For some "respectable," middle-class, Irish-Americans, the struggle is an embarrassment. Becoming informed about injustices or active in their resolution may brand one a supporter of "terrorists" by friends, family, and neighbors.

Young Irish-Americans incur less prejudice than did their ancestors. More socially secure, it may be easier for them to nurture their Irishness. Pride in their own ethnic background may allow them to feel more comfortable with themselves and less threatened by the lingering remnants of anti-Irish Catholicism. It may also enrich their lives with a sense of identity and belonging in a society that seems to grow more rootless. Being informed and assured about their own socio-historical experience may encourage a greater acceptance of differences in others and promote more tolerance. An appreciation of cultural variation may promote intercultural understanding and sensitivity to the needs and aspirations of other groups.

Irish traditional music is performed across the state. Here Tommy O'Halloran and Terry Murphy entertain at the Tipperary Pub in Southfield. Courtesy of the Tipperary Pub.

The oppressive historical roots of the Irish in both Ireland and nineteenth-century America are important to understand in gaining an appreciation for their concern with socio-economic status. The influence of Catholic values on personal values and social attitudes is deep and significant. Further, the historic role of Democratic Party politics and union struggles must be appreciated to understand the socio-political attitudes of many Irish-Americans toward contemporary problems.

Today, Michigan Irish-American cultural activities flourish. Irish language and dance classes are popular across the state. Detroit is home to several schools of Irish dance and can long boast that its own Tim O'Hare was the second Irish-American to win the World Championship in Irish dancing (Michael Flatley of Chicago and Riverdance fame being the first). Irish American cultural organizations like the Ancient Order of Hibernians, Friendly Sons of St. Patrick, the Knights of Equity, and the Irish American Cultural Institute are active. St. Patrick's Day parades and many other festivals are well attended. A variety of pubs and venues offer Irish music, while singing groups from Ireland regularly appear across the state from Conklin to Detroit and Saginaw to Traverse City.

Traditional foods such as Irish soda bread, bacon, sausages, boxty, colcannon, black pudding, and bannock bread grace the tables in Irish-American homes and at their social gatherings. Irish-Americans read Irish literature from Yeats, Joyce, and Shaw to the modern works of Maeve Binchy and the poetry and essays of Bobby Sands. They study Irish history and genealogy and some regularly travel to Ireland. Irish neighborhoods may have disappeared, but a strong sense of Irish identity remains.

Resources for the Irish in Michigan

Most organizations without a mailing address can be located on line.

Genealogical Organizations

- Detroit Society for Genealogical Research, Inc., c/o Burton Historical Collection, Detroit Public Library, 5201 Woodward Ave., Detroit, MI 48202
- Irish Genealogical Society of Michigan, c/o Gaelic League, 2068 Michigan Ave., Detroit, MI 48216

Cultural Organizations

- Ancient Order of Hibernians; Divisions in Wayne County, Otsego County, Lenawee County, Kent County, Oakland County, Macomb County, Grand Traverse County
- Comhaltas Celtoiri Eireann (a.k.a. Detroit Irish Musicians Association)
- Downriver Irish American Club, 1926 West Rd., Trenton, MI 48183
- Daughters of Eireann (Detroit), 65 Brewer Rd., Leonard, MI 48367
- Emerald Society of Detroit (Police)
- Fraternal Order of United Irishman (Detroit)

- Friendly Sons of St. Patrick, 8269 E. Eight Mile Rd., Warren, MI 48089
- Gaelic League of Detroit, 2068 Michigan Ave., Detroit, MI 48216
- Gaelic League of Western Michigan, 30 Parkview Dr. N.E., Grand Rapids, MI 49502
- Irish American Club of Kalamazoo, 125 W. Michigan, Galesburg, MI 49053
- Irish-American Club of Mid-Michigan, P.O. Box 18012, Lansing, MI 48901-8012
- Irish American Club of St. Clair County, 205 Huron Ave., Port Huron, MI 48060
- Irish American Cultural Institute, 4193 Biddle, Wayne, MI 48184
- Irish Heritage Society (Grand Rapids), 2055 28th St. S.E., Grand Rapids, MI 49508-1582
- Knights of Equity (Detroit), 65 Brewer Rd., Leonard, MI 48367
- Ladies Ancient Order of Hibernian (3 divisions)
- Muskegon Irish American Society, 1086 Ireland Ave., Muskegon, MI 49441
- United Irish Societies (Detroit), 2068 Michigan Ave., Detroit, MI 48216

Political Organizations

- Irish American Unity Conference, 22241 Miami, Grosse Isle, MI 48138
- Irish Northern Aid Committee, 14118 Fairmount, Detroit, MI 48932

Dance Schools

- Donahue School of Irish Dance (Grand Rapids), (616) 956-5613
- Heinzman School of Irish Dance (Detroit), 9015 Iowa, Livonia, MI 48150; (734) 762-0997
- O'Hare School of Irish Dance (Detroit), (734) 451-3696

Gaelic Sports

- Padraig Pearse Club, Gaelic Athletic Association, 2068 Michigan Ave., Detroit, MI 48216

Festivals

- The Detroit Feis
- The Gaelic League Festival (Detroit)
- The Great Lakes Irish Music Festival (Muskegon)

Libraries and Archives

- Archive of the Archdiocese of Detroit, 1234 Washington Blvd, Detroit, MI 48226-1875
- Beaver Island Historical Society, 26275 Main St., Beaver Island, MI 49782
- Burton Historical Collection, Detroit Public Library, 5201 Woodward Ave., Detroit, MI 48202; (313) 833-1480
- Copper Country Historical Collections, J.R. Van Pelt Library, Michigan Technological University, 1400 Townsend Dr., Houghton, MI 49931-1295; (906) 487-3209
- State Archives of Michigan, Michigan Library and Historical Center, 717 W. Allegan St., Lansing, MI 48918-1837; (517) 373-1400
- Walter Reuther Library, Wayne State University, 5401 Cass Ave., Detroit, MI 48202

Videos

- *May the Road Rise Up to Melt You:* The Irish Journey to Detroit. United Irish Societies. 2000.
- *Beaver Island: A Video Memento.* Beaver Island Boat Company, Charlevoix, MI.

Music

- *Comhaltas Celtoiri Eireann* (Detroit) (music classes)
- *Fenians Pub* (Conklin, Mich.) (live performances)
- Gaelic League (Detroit) (live performances)
- *Tipperary Pub* (Detroit) (live performances)

Irish Language Classes

- Fenians Pub (Conklin, Mich.) (music and language), 19683 Main St., Conklin, MI 49503
- Gaelic League (Detroit), 2068 Michigan Ave., Detroit, MI 48216

Irish Import Stores

- American Irish Pride, Davison, MI; (810) 658-7917
- America's Emerald Isle Imports, Beaver Island, MI; (616) 448-2800
- Ard-Righ Irish Imports, Saugatuck, MI; (616) 628-5352
- Celtic Fields, Inc., Grand Rapids, MI; (616) 949-5506
- Celtic Gardens Imports, Ann Arbor, MI; (734) 997-9499
- The Celtic Connection, Lake Orion, MI; (248) 393-4466
- Celtic Seasons, Mattawan, MI; (616) 668-8069
- The Celtic Shamrock, Farmington, MI; (248) 615-1804
- The Irish Baker, Livonia, MI; (313) 584-2444
- The Irish Connection, Stanton, MI; (773) 528-5854
- Irish Expectations, Fenton, MI; (810) 750-7070
- The Irish Rose Linen Shop, Port Huron, MI; (810) 982-5487
- Irish Store, New Buffalo, MI; (616) 469-2757
- The Jaunting Cart Ltd., Mackinac Island, MI; (906) 847-6572
- The Leprechaun Shop, Clare, MI; (517) 386-7599
- O'Leary's Tea Room Unlimited, Detroit, MI; (313) 964-0936
- Out of Ireland, Ann Arbor, MI; (734) 973-2709
- Quinlan's Irish Gifts, Davisburg, MI; (248) 634-8804
- Sullivan's Irish Alley Inc., Flushing, MI; (810) 487-2473

Catholic Parishes in Michigan with an Irish or Heavily Irish Origin

Eastern

Adrian, *St. Mary of Good Counsel*

Alpena, *St. Bernard*

Ann Arbor, *St. Thomas*

Bay City, *St. James*

Brighton, *St. Patrick (Green Oak)*

Bunker Hill, *St. Patrick*

Chelsea, *St. Mary*

Cambridge Center, *St. Joseph*

Carlton (Stony Creek), *St. Patrick*

Croswell, *St. Patrick*

Dearborn, *Sacred Heart*

Deerfield, *St. Augustine*

Detroit, *Holy Trinity, St. Vincent de Paul, St. Peter & Paul, St. Brigid Our Lady of Help, St. Aloysius, St. Patrick St. Cecilia St. Gregory Holy Redeemer St. Leo*

Dexter, *St. Joseph*

Emmet (Kenockee), *Our Lady of Mt. Carmel*

Fentonville, *St. John*

Ferndale, *St. James*

Flint, *St. Michael*
Hillsdale, *St. Anthony*
Hubbardston, *St. John the Baptist*
Hudson, *Sacred Heart*
Ionia, *SS. Peter and Paul*
Jackson, *St. John*
Lansing, *St. Mary*
Lapeer, *Immaculate Conception*
Lexington, *Immaculate Conception*
Merrill, *St. Patrick*
Midland, *St. Brigid*
Milford, *St. Mary*
Milan, *Immaculate Conception*
Monroe, *St. John*
Mount Pleasant, *Sacred Heart*
Northfield, *St. Patrick*
Owosso, *St. Paul*
Palms, *St. Patrick*
Pinckney, *St. Mary*
Pontiac, *St. Vincent*
Port Huron, *St. Stephen*
Redford, *St. Mary*
Rosebush, *St. Henry*
Royal Oak, *St. Mary*
Royal Oak, *Shrine of the Little Flower*
Saginaw, *St. Andrew, St. Joseph*
Seville, *St. Patrick (Irishtown)*
Shepherd, *St. Patrick*
Sherman, *SS. Peter and Paul*
Utica, *St. Lawrence*
Wyandotte, *St. Joseph*
Wyandotte, *St. Patrick*
Ypsilanti, *St. John*

Western

Battle Creek, *St. Philip*
Beaver Island, *Holy Cross*
Bowne, *St. Mary*
Cascade, *St. Mary*
Cheboygan, *St. Mary*
Coldwater, *St. Charles*
Grand Haven, *St. Patrick*
Grand Rapids, *St. Andrew, St. James*
Kalamazoo, *St. Augustine*
Manton, *St. Theresa*
Marne (Berlin), *St. Mary*
Marshall, *Immaculate Conception*
Muskegon, *St. Mary*
Niles, *Immaculate Conception*
Otsego, *St. Margaret*
Parnell (Grattan), *St. Patrick*
Paw Paw, *St. Mary*
Plainwell, *St. Agnes*
Silver Creek, *Sacred Heart*
St. Joseph, *St. Joseph*
Watson Township, *Sacred Heart*

Upper Peninsula

Clifton, *Our Lady of the Assumption*
Eagle Harbor, *Holy Redeemer*
Escanaba, *St. Patrick*
Hancock, *St. Ann (later St. Patrick)*
Houghton, *St. Ignatius*
Rockland, *St. Mary*

Irish Ethnic Specialties

rish-Americans continue to prepare and use traditional Irish foods such as colcannon, soda bread, scones, wheaten bannock bread, boxty, black pudding, white pudding, and Irish sausage. What follows are recipes for three Irish ethnic foods.

Colcannon

6 large potatoes
6 scallions
1 cup milk
2 cups steamed cabbage or kale
3–4 Tbsp. melted butter
1 Tbsp. parsley
salt and pepper to taste

Boil and mash potatoes. Chop scallions using green tops and the tender bulbs. The green tops will lend the dish color. To preserve their green hue, scald them by pouring boiling water over them. Drain well. Add scallions to milk and bring to a boil. Mix into potatoes. Beat until fluffy. Toss cabbage or kale in melted butter. Fold into potatoes along with the parsley. Season. Serve welled in the center so that a pat of butter may be added.

Colcannon can be served at any time, but it is traditional to add charms (a coin, ring, thimble, and button) and serve it at Halloween. The charms are individually wrapped in paper and placed in the mixture. They foretell the future of those who find them on their plate. A coin denotes wealth, a ring marriage, a thimble spinsterhood, and a button bachelorhood.

Wheaten Bannock Bread

> 2 cups whole wheat flour
> 1 cup white flour
> ½ tsp. salt
> 1 tsp. baking powder
> 1½ tsp. baking soda
> 2–3 Tbsp. sugar (optional)
> 1½ tsp. butter (optional; the butter will give the bread a
>   brittle texture)
> 1 egg
> 1½ cups buttermilk

Mix the dry ingredients. If using, add butter in small pieces and rub into mixture. Add the egg and buttermilk and mix. Knead on a floured surface. Place the round loaf on a greased baking sheet. Flatten to form 1½" thick round. With a knife, cut a cross into the top. Bake at 375°F for 45 minutes.

Scones

> 4 cups flour
> 1½ tsp. baking powder
> ½ tsp. salt
> 3–4 Tbsp. sugar
> ½ cup butter

1 egg

1 cup milk

In a bowl rub butter into the dry ingredients. With a fork lightly beat the egg and milk together. Add to dry ingredients. Mix lightly and quickly. On a floured surface, roll out the dough to 1" thickness. Cut into rounds with a floured glass bottle or cookie cutter. Bake on lightly floured baking sheet at 400°F approximately 15 min. Cut in two and serve with butter and jam.

Other Important Ethnic Foods

- Soda Bread
- Black Pudding
- White Pudding
- Irish Bacon (rashers)
- Irish Sausage: Bangers (large size); Breakfast sausage (small size)

Notes

1. M. E. Fitzgerald and J. A. King, *The Uncounted Irish in Canada and the United States* (Toronto: PD Meany, 1990), 260.

2. W. F. Dunbar and G. S. May, *Michigan: A History of the Wolverine State* (Grand Rapids, Michigan: Eerdmans, 1995), 244.

3. H. H. Ellis "Robertson's Michigan in War: A Review Article," *Michigan History* 50 (1966): 184.

4. W. D. Griffin, *The Book of Irish Americans* (New York: Random House, 1990), 86.

5. H. Hatcher, *The Great Lakes* (New York: Oxford University Press, 1944), 264.

6. Ibid., 267–68.

7. Ibid., 253.

8. United Irish Societies, *Modern Journeys: The Irish in Detroit* (Detroit: United Irish Societies, 2001), viii.

9. Ibid., 1.

10. H. Hatcher and E. Walter, *A Pictorial History of the Great Lakes* (New York: Crown Publishers, 1963), 212.

11. G. Paré, *The Catholic Church in Detroit, 1701–1888* (Detroit: Published for the Archdiocese of Detroit by Wayne State University Press, 1983), 473.

12. D. O'Brien, *Memoir of the Late Honorable Richard Robert Elliott*, Michigan Pioneer and Historical Reflections (1909–1910), 645.

13. J. E. Vinyard, *The Irish on the Urban Frontier: Nineteenth Century Detroit, 1850–1880* (New York: Arno Press, 1976), 61.

14. T. Sowell, *Ethnic America: A History* (New York: Basic Books, 1981), 27.

15. S. Lebergott, *Manpower in Economic Growth* (New York: McGraw-Hill, 1964), 299, 542.

16. Vinyard, *The Irish*, 58.

17. United Irish Societies, *Modern Journeys*, 14.

18. Paré, *The Catholic Church*, 520.

19. R. Elliott, "First Irish Catholic Parochial Organization Established in the Western States," *American Catholic Historical Researches* 12 (1895): 130.

20. M. Kundig, *Exposition of Facts Relating to Certain Charitable Institutions Within the State of Michigan* (Detroit: E. A. Theller, 1840), 27.

21. Elliott, "First Irish Catholic Parochial Organization," 132, 134.

22. Paré, *The Catholic Church*, 520.

23. United Irish Societies, *Modern Journeys*, 17.

24. Paré, *The Catholic Church*, 463.

25. Vinyard, *The Irish*, 221.

26. S. Metress, *The American-Irish: From Oppression to Freedom* (Toledo, Ohio: University of Toledo, 2002), 72.

27. F. Williams, *Michigan Soldiers in the Civil War* (Lansing, Michigan: Michigan Historical Commission, 1976), 50–55; F. Woodford and A. Woodford, *All Our Yesterdays: A Brief History of Detroit* (Detroit: Wayne State University Press, 1969), 183–84.

28. Ibid., 202.

29. Vinyard, *The Irish*, 157; Woodford and Woodford, *All Our Yesterdays*, 208.

30. Vinyard, *The Irish*, 140.

31. R. Oestreicher, *Solidarity and Fragmentation: Working People and Class Consciousness in Detroit, 1875–1900* (Urbana: University of Illinois Press, 1986), 182.

32. S. Babson, "British and Irish Militants in the Detroit UAW in the 1930s," in *Labor Divided: Race and Ethnicity in United States Labor Struggles 1835–1960*, edited by R. Asher and C. Stephenson (Albany: State University of New York Press, 19900, 243.

33. Babson, "British and Irish Militants," 228; S. Babson, *Building the Union: Skilled Workers and Anglo-Gaelic Immigrants in the Rise of the UAW* (New Brunswick: Rutgers University Press, 1991), 184.

34. Babson, *Building the Union,* 75–76.

35. Woodford and Woodford, *All Our Yesterdays,* 327.

36. Babson, *Building the Union,* 218.

37. K. Boyle, *After the Rainbow Sign: Jerome Cavanaugh and 1960s Detroit.* Detroit: Walter P. Reuther Library, Wayne State University, 2001), 2–3.

38. United Irish Societies, *Modern Journeys,* 21.

39. C. W. Vanderhill, *Settling of the Great Lakes Frontier: Immigration to Michigan, 1837–1924* (Lansing, Michigan: The Sons of Erin, Michigan Historical Commission, 1970), 44.

40. United Irish Societies, *Modern Journeys,* 63.

41. W. Cashman, "The Rise and Fall of the Fishing Industry," *The Journal of Beaver Island History* 1 (1976): 70.

42. J. Runberg, "Boat Building and Builders on the Islands, 1873–1939," *Journal of Beaver Island History* 3 (1988):145.

43. Cashman, "The Rise and Fall," 73.

44. H. Collar, "Irish Migration to Beaver Island," *The Journal of Beaver Island History* 1 (1976): 140.

45. Ibid., 33.

46. Ibid., 47.

47. L. Malloy, *St. Ignatius: A Paper on File* (St. James Beaver Island: Holy Cross Rectory, 1943), 3.

48. L. K. Sommers, *Beaver Island House Party* (St. James, Michigan: Michigan State University Press and The Beaver Island Historical Society, 1996), 24.

49. G. A. Hendrix, "The Songs of Beaver Island," *The Journal of Beaver Island History* 2 (1980): 59.

50. Sommers, *Beaver Island House Party,* 24.

51. W. H. Mulligan Jr., "Irish Immigrants in Michigan Copper County," *New Hibernia Review* 5 no. 4 (2001): 113.

52. T. M. O'Neil, "Miners Migration: The Case of nineteenth Century Irish and Irish American Copper Miners," *Eire/Ireland* 36 nos. 1 and 2 (2001): 130.

53. L. Lankton, *Cradle to the Grave: Life, Work and Death at the Lake Superior Copper Mines* (New York: Oxford University Press, 1991), 20.

54. O'Neil, "Miners Migration," 131, 136.

55. Ibid., 132.

56. A. C. Todd, *The Cornish Miner in America* (Glendale, Calif.: Arthur and Clark, 1967), 242.

57. O'Neil, "Miners Migration," 133.

58. Mulligan, "Irish Immigrants," 120.

59. Ibid., 110.

60. Ibid.

61. J. T. Ridge, *Erin's Sons in America: The Ancient Order of Hibernians* (New York: AOH Publications, 1986), 95.

62. A. W. Thurner, *Calumet Copper and People: History of a Michigan Mining Community, 1864–1970* (Chicago, 1974), 27.

63. Mulligan, "Irish Immigrants," 120.

64. O'Neil, "Miners Migration," 137.

65. W. R. Dunbar, *Michigan: A History of the Wolverine State* (Grand Rapids, Michigan: William B. Eerdmans, 1970), 305–8.

66. J. M. Dickinson, *To Build a Canal: Sault St. Marie, 1853–1854 and After* (Columbus: Published for the Miami University by the Ohio State University of Press, 1981), 81.

67. Dunbar, *Michigan,* 309.

68. T. P. Hennings, *From the Marshgrass: A History of St. Patricks of Northfield* (Northfield: St. Patricks, 1981), 1.

69. Ibid., 4.

70. L. W. Doll, *The History of St. Thomas Parish, Ann Arbor* (Ann Arbor, Mich.: Ann Arbor Press, 1941), 11.

71. Ibid., 23.

72. Ibid., 168.

73. Ibid., 22.

74. O. W. Stephenson, *Ann Arbor: The First Hundred Years* (Ann Arbor, Mich.: Ann Arbor Chamber of Commerce, 1927), 382, 403–4.

75. Doll, *The History of St. Thomas Parish,* 73, 80.

76. R. E. Cross, "Irishtown: A Brief History," in *St. Patrick Irishtown 1868–1968* (Seville Township: St. Patrick's Parish, 1968), 8.

77. A. Baxter, *History of the City of Grand Rapids, Michigan* (New York: Munsell and Company, 1891), 47.

78. C. E. Belknap, *The Yesterdays of Grand Rapids* (Grand Rapids, Mich.: Dean-Hicks, 1922), 44.

79. J. W. McGee, *The Passing of the Gael: Our Irish Ancestors, Their History and Exodus* (Grand Rapids, Michigan: Wolverine Printing Co., 1975), 229.

80. J. W. McGee, *The Catholic Church in the Grand River Valley 1833–1950* (Grand Rapids, Mich., 1950), 206.

81. Ibid., 462.

82. McGee, *The Passing of the Gael*, 286.

83. Ibid., 302.

84. McGee, *The Catholic Church*, 403.

85. McGee, *The Passing of the Gael*, 263.

86. Ibid., 252.

87. McGee, *The Catholic Church*, 419.

88. H. Cusack, *Index of Names, Hubbardston, Yesterday and Today* (Hubbardston, Mich.: Hubbardston Anniversary Committee, 1968), 27.

89. E. L. Sprague and G. N. Smith, *Sprague's History of Grand Traverse and Leelenaw Counties, Michigan* (Traverse City: B. F. Bowen, 1903), 582–83.

90. C. N. Russell and D. D. Baer, *The Lumberman's Legacy* (Manistee, Mich.: The Manistee County Historical Society, 1954), 27.

91. A. M. Greeley, *The Irish Americans: The Rise to Money and Power* (New York: Harper and Row, 1981), 124–25

92. Ibid., 126, 127.

93. M. McGoldrick, J. K. Pearce, and J. Giordano, *Ethnicity and Family Therapy* (New York: Guilford Press, 1982), 320.

94. Ibid., 111.

For Further Reference

Babson, S. "British and Irish Militants in the Detroit UAW in the 1930s." In *Labor Divided: Race and Ethnicity in United States Labor Struggles 1835–1960*, edited by R. Asher and C. Stephenson. Albany: State University of New York Press, 1990.

———. *Building the Union: Skilled Workers and Anglo-Gaelic Immigrants in the Rise of the UAW.* New Brunswick: Rutgers University Press, 1991.

———. "Pointing the Way: The Role of the British and Irish Tradesman in the Rise of the UAW." *Detroit Perspectives* 7 (1983): 75–96.

Baxter, A. *History of the City of Grand Rapids, Michigan.* New York: Munsell and Company, 1891.

Belknap, C. E. *The Yesterdays of Grand Rapids.* Grand Rapids, Mich.: Dean-Hicks, 1922.

Boyle, K. *After the Rainbow Sign: Jerome Cavanaugh and 1960s Detroit.* Detroit: Walter P. Reuther Library, Wayne State University, 2001.

Boyle, M. I. *Early History of the Catholic Church in Saginaw.* University of Notre Dame. Masters Thesis, 1947.

Brown, J. E. "Patriotism or Religion." *Michigan History* 64 (1980):36–42.

Canfield, F. X. "A Diocese So Vast." *Michigan History* 51 (1967):201–12.

Cashman, W. "The Rise and Fall of the Fishing Industry." *The Journal of Beaver Island History* 1 (1976): 69–87.

Collar, H. "Irish Migration to Beaver Island." *The Journal of Beaver Island History* 1 (1976): 27–50.

Crapster, B. L. "New Padua, Justin McCarthy and Ann Arbor." *Michigan History* 42 (1958): 361–66.

Cross, R. E. "Irishtown: A Brief History." In *St. Patrick Irishtown 1868–1968.* Seville Township: St. Patrick's Parish, 1968.

Cusack, H. *Index of Names, Hubbardston Yesterday and Today.* Hubbardston, Michigan: Hubbardston Anniversary Committee, 1968.

Dickinson, J. M. *To Build a Canal: Sault St. Marie, 1853–1854 and After.* Columbus: Published for the Miami University by the Ohio State University of Press, 1981.

Doll, L. W. *The History of St. Thomas Parish, Ann Arbor.* Ann Arbor, Mich.: Ann Arbor Press, 1941.

Dunbar, W. R. *Michigan: A History of the Wolverine State.* Grand Rapids, Michigan: William B. Eerdmans, 1970.

Dunbar, W. F. and G. S. May. *Michigan: A History of the Wolverine State.* Grand Rapids, Michigan: Eerdmans, 1995.

Elliott, R. "First Irish Catholic Parochial Organization Established in the Western States." *American Catholic Historical Researches* 12 (1895): 129–39.

Ellis, H. H. "Robertson's Michigan in War: A Review Article." *Michigan History* 50 (1966): 178–85.

Fitzgerald, M. E. and J. A. King. *The Uncounted Irish in Canada and the United States.* Toronto: P.D. Meany, 1990.

Fitzmaurice, J. F. *The Shanty Boy or Life in a Lumber Camp.* Ann Arbor, 1979 (reprint of 1889 ed.).

Gallagher, H. S. "Beaver Island, Michigan : An Irish Island Colony." *Journal of American Historical Society* 28 (1930): 198–203.

Greeley, A. M. *The Irish Americans: The Rise to Money and Power.* New York: Harper and Row, 1981.

Griffin, W. D. *The Book of Irish Americans.* New York: Random House, 1990.

Hannon, J. U. "Ethnic Discrimination in a Nineteenth-Century Mining District Michigan Copper Mines 1888." *Explorations in Economic History* 18 (1982):28–50.

Hatcher, H. *The Great Lakes.* New York: Oxford University Press, 1944.

Hatcher, H., and E. Walter. *A Pictorial History of the Great Lakes.* New York: Bonanza Books, 1963.

Hayes, F. H. *Michigan Catholicism in the Era of the Civil War.* Lansing, Mich.: Centennial Observance Commission, 1965.

Hendrix, G. A. "An Island of Fiddlers." *Journal of Beaver Island History* 3 (1980): 51–58.

Hendrix, G. A. "Songs of Beaver Island." *The Journal of Beaver Island History* 2 (1980): 59–111.

Hennings, T. P. *From the Marshgrass: A History of St. Patricks of Northfield.* Northfield: St. Patricks, 1981.

Janis, R. *The Churches of Detroit: A Study in Urban Social Structure 1880–1940.* University of Michigan. Ph.D. Dissertation, 1972.

———. "Ethnic Mixture and the Persistence of Cultural Pluralism in the Church Communities of Detroit, 1880–1940." *Mid-America* 61, no. 2 (1979): 99–115.

King, J. A. *The Irish Lumberman-farmer: Fitzgeralds, Harrigans, and Others.* Lafayette, Calif.: K & K Publications, 1982.

Kinzer, D. "The Political Users of Anti-Catholicism: Michigan and Wisconsin, 1890–1894." *Michigan History.* 39 (1955):312–326.

Kundig, M. *Exposition of Facts Relating to Certain Charitable Institutions Within the State of Michigan.* Detroit: E. A. Theller, 1840.

Lankton, L. *Cradle to Grave: Life, Work and Death at the Lake Superior Copper Mines.* New York: Oxford University Press, 1991.

Lebergott, S. *Manpower in Economic Growth.* New York: McGraw-Hill, 1964.

Malloy, L. *St. Ignatius: A Paper on File.* St. James Beaver Island: Holy Cross Rectory, 1943.

Marman, E. ed. *Modern Journey: the Irish in Detroit.* Detroit: United Irish Societies, 2001.

McGee, J. W. *The Catholic Church in the Grand River Valley 1833–1950.* Grand Rapids, Mich., 1950.

McGee, J. W. *The Passing of the Gael: Our Irish Ancestors, Their History and Exodus.* Grand Rapids, Mich.: Wolverine Print Co., 1975.

McGowan, B. K. *Historical and Ethnic Retention of Irish Republicanism in a Large Mid-Western City.* Wayne State University. Ph.D. Dissertation, 1994.

Metress, S. *The American-Irish: From Oppression to Freedom.* Toledo, Ohio: University of Toledo, 2002.

Mulligan, W. H., Jr. "Irish Immigrants in Michigan Copper County." *New Hibernia Review* 5 no. 4 (2001): 109–22.

Murdoch, A. *Boom Copper: The Story of the First U.S. Mining Boom.* New York:

The Macmillan Company, 1943 (reprinted in 1964).

O'Brien, D. *Memoir of the Late Honorable Richard Robert Elliott.* 1909–1910. Michigan Pioneer and Historical Collections 37: 645–59.

O'Neil, T. M. "Miners Migration: The Case of Nineteenth Century Irish and Irish American Copper Miners." *Eire/Ireland* 36 nos. 1 and 2 (2001): 124–141.

Oestreicher, R. *Solidarity and Fragmentation: Working People and Class Consciousness in Detroit, 1875–1900.* Urbana: University of Illinois Press, 1986.

Paré, G. *The Catholic Church in Detroit, 1701–1888.* Detroit: Published for the Archdiocese of Detroit by Wayne State University Press, 1983.

Ridge, J. T. *Erin's Sons in America: The Ancient Order of Hibernians.* New York: AOH Publications, 1986.

Riordan, J. J. *The Dark Peninsula.* Au Train, Mich.: Avery Color Studies, 1981.

Runberg, J. "Boat Building and Builders on the Islands, 1873–1939." *Journal of Beaver Island History* 3 (1988): 143–60.

Russell, C. N. and D. D. Baer. *The Lumberman's Legacy.* Manistee, Michigan: The Manistee County Historical Society, 1954.

Sommers, L. K. *Beaver Island House Party.* East Lansing: Michigan State University Press and The Beaver Island Historical Society, 1996.

Sowell, T. *Ethnic America: A History.* New York: Basic Books, 1981.

Sprague, E. L. and G. N. Smith. *Sprague's History of Grand Traverse and Leelenaw Counties, Michigan.* Traverse City: B. F. Bowen, 1903.

Stack, R. E. . *The McCleers and the Barneys: Irish Immigrant Families Into Michigan and the California Goldfields, 1820–1893.* St. Louis University. Ph.D. Dissertation, 1972.

Stephenson, O. W. *Ann Arbor: The First Hundred Years.* Ann Arbor, Mich.: Ann Arbor Chamber of Commerce, 1927.

Tentler, L. W. *Seasons of Grace: A History of the Catholic Diocese of Detroit.* Detroit: Wayne State University, 1990.

Thurner, A. W. *Calumet Copper and People: History of a Michigan Mining Community, 1864–1970.* Chicago, 1974.

Todd, A. C. *The Cornish Miner in America.* Glendale, Calif.: Clark, 1967.

United Irish Societies. *Modern Journeys: The Irish in Detroit.* Detroit: United Irish Societies, 2001.

Vanderhill, C. W. *Settling of the Great Lakes Frontier: Immigration to Michigan,*

1837–1924. Lansing, Michigan: The Sons of Erin, Michigan Historical Commission, 1970.

Vinyard, J. E. *For Faith and Fortune: The Education of Catholic Immigrants in Detroit, 1805–1925.* Urbana: University of Illinois Press, 1998.

———. "Inland Urban Immigrants: the Detroit Irish 1850." *Michigan History* 57 (1974):121–139.

———. *The Irish on the Urban Frontier: Detroit 1850–1880.* University of Michigan. Ph.D. Dissertation, 1972 (reprinted 1976, New York: Arno Press).

———. *The Irish on the Urban Frontier: Nineteenth Century Detroit, 1850–1880.* New York: Arno Press, 1976.

Williams, F. *Michigan Soldiers in the Civil War.* Lansing, Michigan: Michigan Historical Commission, 1976.

Woodford, F. and A. Woodford. *All Our Yesterdays: A Brief History of Detroit.* Detroit: Wayne State University Press, 1969.

Zunz, O. "The Organization of the American City in the Late Nineteenth Century: Ethnic Structure and Spatial Arrangement in Detroit." *Journal of Urban History.* 3, no. 4 (1977):443–66.

Index